THE VIOLA

THE VIOLA: COMPLETE GUIDE FOR TEACHERS AND STUDENTS

by

HENRY BARRETT

The University of Alabama Press
University, Alabama

FOREWORD

Prior to preparing this volume the writer received, by means of a question-naire, pertinent data on the state of viola instruction in America. Over two hundred and fifty teachers of viola who are members of the American String Teachers Association were asked to supply information concerning current practice, specific problems, standards of performance, special techniques in use, causes for dropouts, and job opportunities in all parts of the country. Open-end in construction to encourage discussion, the questionnaire brought to light some interesting information on the current status of viola pedagogy. References to the practices of viola teachers in the United States made throughout this volume were determined by the information drawn from this survey.

An interesting discovery, supporting the writer's belief in the need for this study, is the fact that most of the teaching of viola is undertaken by violinists who have little or no experience in playing the viola, who have only a perfunctory knowledge of the literature, and who are the first to confess their limitations. It is to the solution of the problems enumerated by these teachers that this book is addressed.

The author wishes to acknowledge his indebtedness to the Research Grants Committee of the University of Alabama for financial assistance during the writing of this volume and to his friends—artist Richard Brough, theorist Steve Sample, and photographer Andy Russell—for their invaluable services.

CONTENTS

THE VIOLA

Chapter I

LITERATURE FOR VIOLA

Over 1500 works have been published featuring the viola in a solo role. This total continues to increase year by year at an amazing rate. The viola music currently available in print includes at least 190 concertos, 300 sonatas, 650 solo pieces, 250 studies, and 40 albums of pieces. While a significant portion of this music is transcribed from the literature of other instruments, enough original works for viola are available to satisfy the purist. Only music of the Classical and Romantic periods is deficient in quantity, a shortcoming that may be partially eliminate'd in the future. The reference works of Eitner[1] and Altmann[2] list scores of classical compositions for viola that are unpublished or out of print.

To delve into the history of the viola, in search of factors leading to its neglect, is to encounter conflicting terminology and confused ancestry. As early as the fifteenth century the term viola (literally "with the bow") was used by Tinctoris to define a three or five stringed fiddle used for public festivities. In the sixteenth century, viola was used generically to label any member of either the viol (viola da gamba) or the violin families (viola da braccio). Occasionally the term was used to refer to the "lira da braccio," considered along with the rebec and Renaissance fiddle as ancestors of the modern stringed family.

To search the ancient viols for a common ancestral root of the modern viola is to look in vain. The characteristics of the viols are the antithesis of the structural features of the modern viola: fretted fingerboard; flatter bridge; sloping shoulders; flat back; deep ribs; plain corners at the bouts; C-shaped sound-holes; six strings tuned in fourths; and thin wood producing a soft, silvery tone.

The new violin family of the early sixteenth century combined the best features of many bowed predecessors and owed, therefore, a debt to the following: the Lira da braccio for its shallow body and moulded back; the Rebec for its peg box and tuning in fifths; the Fiedel for its rounded bridge and cornered bouts; and the Vielle for F-shaped sound holes.

---

[1]Eitner, Robert. *Biographisch-bibliographisches Quellen-Lexikon der Musiker und Musikgelehrten der Christlicken Zeitrechnung bis zur Mitte des 19. Jahrhundertis.* Leipzig, Breitkopf & Hartel, 1900-04.

[2]Altmann, Wilhelm & W. Borissowsky. *Literaturverzeichnis für Bratsche und Viola d'amore.* Wolfenbüttel, Verlag für musikalische Kultur & Wissenschaft, 1937.

The dearth of viola music in the eighteenth and nineteenth centuries may be attributed to a low prestige point in the history of the instrument. The viola, in the form of the viola da braccio, had figured prominently in the instrumental music of the sixteenth and seventeenth centuries, although no great technical demands were made of the performers. With the advent of the "golden age" of the violin, the viola was pushed into the background in instrumental ensembles and denied its fair share of solo string literature for the next two centuries.

The decline in popularity during this period was due not only to the ascendancy of the violin as an accoustically perfect instrument, but to inherent weakness in the viola itself. Early violas were constructed with short necks in proportion to their size, making position playing extremely difficult, if not impossible. Further, oversized violas of the day greatly restricted the player's technical dexterity and limited composers' efforts to exploit the instrument's resources. The situation did have the positive effect of hastening experimentation on the dimensions of the instrument, an evolution that has not run its course to this day.

Although the future of the instrument was uncertain, a few composers of stature made invaluable contributions to the solo viola literature, perhaps looking forward to the day when highly gifted musicians would devote their lives to establishing the viola as a solo instrument of unmatched beauty. Telemann (1681-1767) wrote the first concerto for the instrument as well as giving it a major role in his other compositions. Stamitz, Mozart, Dittersdorf, Rolla, and Hoffmeister provided the violist with master works in the eighteenth and early nineteenth centuries. Solo compositions by Beethoven, Brahms, Berlioz, and Schumann complete the nineteenth century and bring the violist to more fertile fields. Only in the twentieth century is a virtually unlimited repertory available.

TRANSCRIPTIONS

Inasmuch as a large part of viola music in print consists of transcriptions, consideration of the ethics of the procedure may be a logical starting point in a general overview of the printed music available to teachers and students. The case for transcriptions has been strengthened by composers themselves. Consider J. S. Bach's E Major Partita for violin alone. The venerated contrapuntalist transposed his work to the key of D, scored it for organ, three trumpets, and strings, and renamed it Sinfonia to use in his Church Cantata no. 29. Beethoven, feeling the financial pressure of free lancing, sanctioned the transcriptions of several of his works including the String Trio, op. 8, by composers of lesser stature. The new version of the Trio, retitled Notturno for viola and piano, was so poor that the work disappeared entirely from publishers' catalogues late in the nineteenth century. Recent transcriptions of the Notturno reflect better writing for the keyboard and a more soloistic treatment of the viola line, helping fill a conspicuous void in the viola music of this period.

With the precedent well established before them, Shore and Westcott transcribed the Bach *Praeludium* for viola and piano while Carlton Cooley reworked the Prelude and Gigue from Bach's Suite no. 6 and Maurice Johnstone arranged three movements of Suite no. 1 for the same instruments. These transcriptions come off quite well in performance, a bonus point in justification of "borrowed" music, but the Kodály arrangement of Bach's *Fantasia Chromatica* for viola solo suffers in comparison to the original in a general lack of resonance. The arpeggiated passages are realization of chords in the harpsichord score and give the work, at quick glance, a startling resemblance to the Paganini *Caprices*.

Many violists reject, in toto, transcriptions of the Bach sonatas for violin as being not suited to their instruments. Many masterworks, traditionally associated with their assigned instruments, should be left in their natural state. The challenge of attempting to duplicate either the brilliance of the violin in a transcription of the Wieniawski Concerto no. 2 or the sonority of the cello in a rewrite of the Dvorak Concerto may be attempting the impossible. The practice of mind over matter can only be taken to reasonable limits.

Another arrangement that comes off the worse for the attempt is the Chester publication of the Mozart Concerto for Clarinet. Over fifty measures were cut from the first movement, deftly removing the closing theme, which in turn made the final section badly out of balance. The rondo movement lost an additional hundred bars including much of the composer's interesting chromatic progressions. Mozart's sense of form was too acute to permit such drastic surgery.

Of the modern string family the viola most nearly matches the viola da gamba in tone quality, justifying full exploration of this source of important masterworks. Transcriptions of Bach's three sonatas for viola da gamba are extremely violistic, fair game for the performer seeking to extend his Baroque repertoire. The second of the set is most often performed, with the third sonata a close rival in popularity.

A deciding factor in the acceptance of many transcriptions is the degree of transparency of the accompaniment. Regardless of how idiomatic the writing may be, the performer should not be required to fight for his life on the concert stage. How many pianists, during a viola recital, have thoughts only for their colleagues in the audience or for their future prospects for soloing with the Philharmonic? A sensitive pianist is to be valued as highly as a collection of transcriptions from the Classical period.

The single greatest effort in extending the violist's repertory has been made by Lionel Tertis, the great English violist, whose life has been dedicated to the promotion of his chosen instrument. Following in his footsteps are two musical giants whose works always exhibit impeccable taste, William Primrose and Paul Doktor. They have tapped particularly rich resources. Their transcriptions may be accepted without question.

A summary of selected transcriptions of major works that are highly idiomatic and admired by performer and listener alike is a revelation of the expanded horizon of the twentieth century violist. For the many other transcriptions available in print, see all sections of the Appendix.

Selected Transcriptions of Major Works

Composer	Title	Original Medium
Ariosti	2 Sonatas	Viola d'amore
J. S. Bach	6 Suites	Violoncello
K. P. E. Bach	Concerto in A	Violoncello
Beethoven	2 Romances	Violin
Borodin	Nocturne and Scherzo	String Quartet
Handel	6 Sonatas	Violin and Viola da gamba
Haydn	Concerto in D	Violoncello
Marcello	6 Sonatas	Violin
Paganini	24 Caprices	Violin
Porpora	2 Sonatas	Violin
Schumann	Adagio and Allegro	Horn
Tchaikowsky	Variations on a Rococo Theme	Violoncello
Telemann	12 Fantasias	Violin
Vivaldi	4 Concertos	Violin and Viola d'amore
Vivaldi	6 Sonatas	Violoncello

ORIGINAL MUSIC FOR VIOLA

Some of the earliest examples of original music for viola may be found in the works of Marin Marais (1656-1728) and William Flacton (1709-1798). Marais' compositions exhibit a rare Gallic charm and require of the player a feeling for style and more than a minimum technique.

The Flacton sonatas are rewarding works. An earlier publication of Doblinger identified the composer of the C Major, D Major, and G Major Sonatas as anonymous but this error has been rectified. The canonic Siciliana from the Sonata in C stands out as a particularly beautiful movement.

The two concertos assigned to Handel are suspect, to say the least. Violists commonly agree that Casadesus wrote the B Minor while John Barbirolli put together five movements from "diverse and little known sources" to form the other.

At first glance the violist may not recognize Mozart as a patron of his instrument, for the facile composer left no solo works for the viola alone. However, his treatment of the instrument in a dozen or more chamber works and in the Sinfonia Concertante is evidence of his revolutionary break with the past. Though the level of viola performance was low at the time, Mozart gave the instrument independent lines of great importance in many major works. Mozart played the viola himself and, in fact, premiered the Trio in E flat, K. 498, which teamed the viola with clarinet and piano.

In the Sinfonia Concertante, the viola matches the violin note for note throughout the three movements, which have many distinguishing features. The first movement contains five principal themes and brings the solo instruments together in octaves, thirds, and sixths and in an antiphonal display of pyro-technics. The C minor Andante is a poignant, plaintive statement that reaches epic proportions and involves intricate canonic writing. The Presto is an irrepressibly joyful chase, which closes with a three-octave triplet figure (Example 1), difficult enough for twentieth-century violists and probably virtually impossible for most eighteenth-century players.

Example 1

Sinfonia Concertante   Mozart

Presto, measures 432–444

Some of the finest, and certainly the most virtuoso, writing for viola occurs in duos with other instruments. Violists must not miss the Wilhelm Friedemann Bach and Karl Stamitz duets for two violas and the Henry Cowell Variations on Thirds for two violas and orchestra. The cello is an agreeable teammate in the Beethoven Duet "With 2 Eyeglasses Obligato," the Milhaud Sonatina and the Piston Duo. However, the really spectacular works pair viola with violin, as in Mozart's 2 Duos, Martinu's 3 Madrigals, the Handel-Halvorsen Sarabande and Passacaglia and the Toch Divertimento. Additional duos are included in the Appendix.

The two sonatas, opus 120, are the final chamber works of Johannes Brahms and sum up, introspectively in the twilight of full maturity, his art and his craft. Though shared in an alternate version with clarinet, these sonatas represent the finest solo writing for viola from any period. The piano score is relatively transparent and at times interweaves polyphonically with the viola line. Other examples showing Brahms' fondness for viola are found in the two beautiful songs, "Gestillte Sehnsucht" set to a poem by Friedrich Ruckert and "Geistliches Wiegenlied" based on a poem by Emanuel Geibel, who in turn borrowed the text from the great Spanish poet Lope de Vega. The latter work is a Christmas song dating back to the fifteenth century that has served as a theme for works by such diverse composers as Liszt, Smetana, Humperdinck, and Reger. In dedicating this song to his friend Joachim, Brahms wrote "you will never discover a more beautiful melody."

Berlioz' *Harold in Italy* was commissioned by Niccolo Paganini, who subsequently rejected it after seeing the score of the first movement. The premiere of the completed work so moved the great virtuoso that he apologized to the composer and made payment, fulfilling his commission. Had Paganini been the violist to stand silently for ten minutes during an orchestra tutti in the final movement, he may have entertained second thoughts about Berlioz's creation. From the audience's point of view this is a popular work without a hint of Tovey's reference to "a multitude of grammatical solecisms."

Soliloquy and Dance by Roy Harris explores the viola's depth and moods, requiring of the player an ability to pace himself for a long period without exposing the full sonority of his instrument. The long line of the Soliloquy moves forward slightly for sixty-eight measures to a high peak before winding down gradually and leading into a dance movement theme of great charm, first stated by the piano (Example 2).

Example 2

Dance, measures 1-7   Harris

Used by permission of G. Schirmer, Inc.

The violist may not fully enjoy this inventive piano statement for he is faced with an entrance on high D following twenty-nine bars rest. To find the D in advance is to immobilize the left hand and may lead to self-doubts. Did the finger move slightly, or did it not? The violist has a choice of tapping the string with the bow, displaying his insecurity to the audience, or dropping his finger sharply to the string hoping that he can match the piano tonality in progress, or, his best choice, a light left hand pizzicato in sixth position with the first finger on G during the final eight bars before the viola entrance. At that point the piano theme centers around G. D is easily found as a standard arpeggio extension; that is, GBD fingered 1-3-4 (Example 3).

Example 3

Dance, measures 30-34   Harris

Used by permission of G. Schirmer, Inc.

Among collections of viola works is a valuable album, the Peters edition, *Alte Meister de Violaspiels,* containing the Stamitz Concerto, four sonatas by

Hammer, including one for viola d'amore, and a virtuoso Allegro Movement by an anonymous composer. Collections of solos by Melvin Berger and Paul Doktor should be in every teacher's library as an invaluable source of teaching pieces. The Augener series, which is extensive, is listed separately in the Appendix.

In many instances contemporary composers have looked to the past for inspiration in utilizing the dark, sombre qualities of the viola which are so suited to the expression of great philosophical truths. Vaughan Williams, inspired by the Song of Solomon, composed *Flos Campi* for solo viola, small chorus, and orchestra. The voices sing neutral syllables throughout while the viola, in improvisatory style, takes the role of the Biblical poet in a most sensual setting.

Benjamin Britten's *Lachrymae; Reflections on a Song of Dowland* is a series of ten variations that begins in the twentieth-century harmonic idiom and regresses to a modal conclusion that is not marked *senza vibrato* but must be played in that way in the final four measures (Example 4). The theme is taken from the *First Book of Airs* of 1597.

Example 4

Lachrymae

Britten

For melodic material Hindemith reached back to the 16th and 17th centuries for four German folk tunes for his concerto, *Der Schwanendreher,* while Milhaud used unedited and anonymous themes of the 18th century for Sonata no. 1. In the last movement of his sonata for viola and piano, Robert Kelderfer uses as a theme a melody from the 1514 *Antwerper Liederbuch.* Kenneth Leighton offers the violist *Fantasia on the Name of Bach* while Johann Nepomuk David finds the same subject appropriate for a fugue in the final Adagio of *Melancholia* (op. 53) for viola and chamber orchestra.

Published music for combinations of instruments that border on the exotic is on the rise. Beginning with Dittersdorf's Concertante for viola, double-bass, and orchestra and by way of Debussy's sonata for flute, viola, and harp, the violist has at his command many stunning works including Partos' *Agada* for viola, piano, and percussion (vibraphone, gongs, drums, and cymbal) and the Variations for four roto-drums and viola by Michael Colgrass. The latter publication, a most effective work of great sensuality, suffers from errors in clef notation. In Variation no. 1 measures 44-53 should read alto clef as should measures 98-101 in the third variation and measures 22-25 and 38-48 in the fourth variation. Bars three and four in Variation no. 2 should read treble clef. A recent recording in the Boston Symphony Chamber Series, perhaps with the composer's blessing, indicates a few cuts, additional notes in the drum score, and an alteration in the viola part in bar 42 of Variation no. 2 to bring the two instruments into unison. Printed in score form, the drum is in the alto clef throughout, a particular aid to the violist.

Karlheinz Stockhausen's *Prozession* for tamtam, viola, electronium, piano, filters, and potentiometers (1967) brings the viola to the world of electronic music, where it loses its identity completely. The violist, equipped with a contact microphone connected to an electric filter and potentiometer, is called on to perform episodes of three earlier works of the composer. All performers react to either their most recent statement or to that of another instrument causing, according to the composer, "chain reactions of imitation, transformation, and mutation." Each performance represents a new version of the work with the players actively involved in the creative process. One essential ingredient that may not be available to the violist is Mr. Stockhausen himself, who trains his ensemble and operates the electronic equipment.

A 1969 publication, *Viopiacem* by Claudio Spies, composed for viola and keyboard instruments, is a facile work in a post-Webern style. One performer mans both piano and harpsichord, turning from one to another, and at the end plays both at once.

Bergsma's *Fantastic Variations on a Theme from Tristan* is a technically difficult work due to wide leaps, octave passages, and the speed of certain sections. Exciting and gratifying to perform, the player is rewarded for his gymnastics with a final pitch "E" on the "A" string held for a total of 57 beats.

Ernest Bloch's *Suite Hebraique* is one of the truly magnificent works for viola, a work in which it earns its reputation as an instrument suited for expressing life's innermost feelings. With the three movements, Rhapsodie, Processional, and Affirmation, William Primrose has recorded Bloch's Meditation and Processional, published separately, as a very effective five-piece group. Bloch's suite for viola and piano is a lengthy work, effectively written. The suite for viola alone comes to a surprise ending in mid-phrase, providing the violist with his "Unfinished Suite." In performance, the player ends at the beginning of the final section.

Edmund Rubbra permits the viola to dominate the orchestra in his Concerto in A, op. 75, an extremely pleasant and accessible work. The first movement has the traditional two themes although marked *Introduzione quasi una fantasia.* An interesting feature is the last movement titled "Collana musicale" or musical necklace. Many independent short sections are laced together, and the tonal colors of the viola are explored in depth throughout.

The concerto by Gyorgy Kurtag is purported to be a further development of Bartók's style and tradition. The piece is well written, challenging for the soloist, and orchestrated to present few difficulties to players of average ability. The new edition of the William Walton concerto (1964) eliminated six instruments, greatly improving the balance of solo and orchestra and the effectiveness of the entire work.

Little-known contemporary works that are well-constructed and show a feeling for the various tone colors of the viola are as follows:

Malcolm Arnold	Sonata
Christopher Edmunds	Four Pieces
Paul Walter Fürst	Sonatina, op. 13
Harald Genzmer	Sonata no. 2
Julius Harrison	Sonata in C Minor
Karl Holler	Sonata in E$^\flat$, op. 62
Maurice Jacobson	Humoresque and Berceuse
Alan Richardson	Intrada
John Wray	Capriccioso

Performers favoring the cyclic treatment of material or the use of a single unifying motive may wish to try sonatas by Arthur Benjamin, Arthur Bliss, Norman Fulton, Paul Hindemith (op. 11, no. 5), and John Joubert, and the concerto of William Walton, to cite a few outstanding examples.

METHODS AND STUDIES

Original methods for viola are available in quantity and are listed with transcribed violin methods under Study Material in the Appendix. Most select studies for viola are in progressive order, phrased, fingered, and arranged. The sources tapped are individual etudes from standard violin works by Campagnoli, Mazas, Kreutzer, Fiorello, Rode, Gaviniès, and others, most of which are published separately in complete form. Excellent collections deserving consideration are those by Berta Volmer and Emil Kreuz. For the extension of technique through the modern idiom, the violist may wish to pursue the etudes of Lillian Fuchs and Elizabeth Green and Lukacs' *Exercises in Change of Position.* Books of studies covering every facet of technique are those by Fischer, Hofmann, Kayser, Bruni, Blumenstengel, Wohlfahrt, Campagnoli, Fiorello, Kreutzer, Palaschko, Rode, and Gaviniès.

Studies concentrated on one phase of technique building, while not numerous, are available, as listed in the Appendix. The Schradieck *School of Viola Technique,* transcribed from the violin work, is limited to intonation studies in Part I, double stops including fingered octaves in Part II, and staccato bowing in Part III. Kreuz, in his *Progressive Studies,* uses only flat keys (major and minor) in Book 2, assigning sharp keys to Book 3. The Pagels transcriptions of Rode and Rovelli are written entirely in the alto clef, providing concentrated reading of ledger lines above the staff. Spaulding's volume, *Viola for Violinists,* is a clear presentation of the first six positions and includes fingerboard charts, theory assignments, and several extended solos for practice purposes.

The Karman edition of Carl Flesch's *Scale System* provides a traditional violin approach to scale study and includes enough double-stop scales to tax the strength of the strongest player. *The Art and Practice of Scale Playing on the Viola* by William Primrose employs a different philosophy of shifting. Most shifts are delegated to the A string, with correspondingly fewer shifts but wider leaps. This system is designed to tap the natural sonorities of the viola and, like all of Mr. Primrose's publications, is carefully edited and highly regarded. For thorough grounding in finger patterns, the reader is encouraged to explore Robert Dolejsi's *Modern Viola Technique* and William Primrose's work *Technique is Memory.*

GRADED LISTS

All graded lists of music are suspect, including this one. The teacher will discover, as did the grader, that few compositions offer equal technical and musical difficulties or require the same degree of development of the left and right hands. It is quite possible to find a composition that could be classified Grade 3, right hand technique, Grade 6, left hand technique, and Grade 8 in musicality. Usually left unanswered are crucial questions about the grading process. Does the graded list suggest the level of performance of the private students of an experienced teacher in a large city or university or the members of the newly formed school orchestra in an isolated community? Do grade levels refer to accomplishments of average or exceptional students? Unsolved still is the problem of selection of music on a basis of each student's interest, capacity, and intent.

It is the author's opinion that most teachers push students too rapidly, introducing new problems before early techniques have been firmly established. For this reason, several compositions have been assigned a lower classification than may be found in other graded lists. For the teacher's guidance, short musical examples have been included illustrating typical levels of difficulty for each grade.

Elementary Level

For the beginning years, the teacher may choose from the many string methods, albums of collected pieces, and transcriptions available for viola. Special consideration should be given the works of the English composers Carse, Forbes, Kreuz, Murray and Tate, Richardson, and others who have helped fill an otherwise sparse area. Their works exhibit an originality and charm lacking in much of the beginning literature. Selection of teaching material should vary with the age and ability of the student and the organization of the class into private or group instruction.

12

Grade One

The introduction of sharped keys with concentration on the two-three finger pattern is favored by most teachers with some work in the one-two pattern late in the first year. The use of rhythmic bowing patterns set to simple folk tunes is strongly recommended. Simple détaché bowing. One octave scales: C, G, D, and F.

Example 5

SERENADE   Beriot-Applebaum

Example 6

QUICK STEPS   Murray-Tate

STUDY MATERIAL

Applebaum	Early Etudes for Strings	Belwin
Applebaum	String Builder, Book 1	Belwin
Best	All Strings	Varitone
Bornoff	Finger Patterns	CF
Bornoff	String Reader	CF
Carse	Viola School, Book 1	Augener
Etling	Workbook for Strings, Book 1	Etling
Fischer	Violin and Viola Calisthenics	Belwin
Gardner	Viola Method, Book 1	BMC
Herfurth	Tune a Day, Book 1	BMC
Herman	Bow and Strings, Book 1	Belwin
Jones-Dasch-Krone	Strings from the Start, Part 1	CF
Kinsey	Easy Progressive Studies for Viola	Mills
Knechtel	Universal's Fundamental Method	Universal
Laoureux-Iotti	Practical Method for Viola	GS
Martin	Funway to Fiddletown	Seraphic
Rubank	Elementary Method	Rubank
Skornika-Moehlmann	Instrumental Course	BH
Whistler-Nord	Beginning Strings, Vol. 1	CF

REPERTORY

Applebaum	Building Technic with Beautiful Music	Belwin
Brown (ed)	Polychordia First Set of Viola Solos	Galaxy
(Collection)	Viola Miniatures	CF
DeBeriot-Applebaum	Serenade	Belwin
Forbes	A First Year Classical Album	Oxford
Hauser	Berceuse	CF
Kesnar	Melodie	CF
Kovacs	Happy Days	CF
Kreuz	Melody	Augener
Kreuz	Pensée fugitive	Augener
Kreuz	Romance	Augener
Lovell	44 Easy Tunes	Oxford
MacDowell-Applebaum	To a Wild Rose	Belwin
Mendelssohn	Venetian Gondola Song	Augener
Murray and Tate	The New Viola Books, Book 1	Oxford
Murray and Tate	Tunes New and Old	Oxford
Rowley	Farandole	Mills
Rowley	Scherzo	Mills
Schlemüller	A Prayer, op. 6	CF
Schumann	Melody and Soldiers' March	Augener
Schumann	Siciliano	Augener
Weber	Air	Augener
Work-Applebaum	Grandfather's Clock	Belwin

Grade Two

Begin the second year by firmly establishing the techniques of the first year. Some second-year methods move too rapidly, covering all keys in the first position. Introduction of third position late in the year is desirable after the left- and right-hand positions have been set. Shifting is introduced more successfully by rote. Emphasize détaché and martelé bowings in different parts of the bow and full-bow legato strokes for tonal development. One octave scales: D, A, E. Two octave scales: C, D.

Example 7

LÄNDLER   Mozart-Carruthers

Example 8

PETITE GAVOTTE   Aletter

STUDY MATERIAL

Applebaum	String Builder, Book 2	Belwin
Carse	Viola School, Book 2	Augener
Etling	Workbook for Strings, Book 2	Etling
Gardner	Viola Method, Book 2	BMC
Herfurth	Tune a Day, Book 2	BMC
Herman	Bow and Strings, Book 2	Belwin
Kreuz	Progressive Studies, op. 40, Book 1	Augener
Kreuz	Select Studies for the Viola, Book 1	Augener
Laoureux-Iotti	Practical Method for the Viola (continue)	
Lifschey	Scale and Arpeggio Studies	GS
Müller (ed)	28 Etudes for Strings	Belwin
Reese (arr)	22 Studies for Strings	Belwin
Ševčik-Lifschey	Selected Studies in the First Position	GS
Skornika-Moehlman	Instrumental Course (continue)	
Whistler	Elementary Scales and Bowings	Rubank
Whistler	Essential Studies	Rubank
Whistler and Hummel	Intermediate Scales and Bowings	Rubank
Wohlfahrt-Hohmann- Hening	22 Studies for Strings	Belwin
Wohlfahrt	Foundation Studies for Viola, Book 1	CF
Wohlfahrt-Vieland	30 Studies, op. 45	International

REPERTORY

Aletter	Melodie	CF
Aletter	Petite Gavotte	CF
Ashton	Two Pieces, Ländler and Tarantella	StB
Boetze (ed)	Viola Music for Concert and Church	BMC
Brodszky	Old Music for Viola	EdM, Kultura
Carse	A Breezy Story	Augener
Clementi-Applebaum	Sonatina	Belwin
Dodgson	4 Fancies	Chappell

Forbes	A Second Year Classical Album For Viola Players	Oxford
Gluck	Air from Orfeo	Augener
Gossec-Isaac-Lewis	Gavotte	CF
Handel	Largo	Augener
Hauser	Cradle Song	CF
Haydn	Air (from The Seasons)	Augener
Herfurth (ed)	Classical Album of Early Grade Pieces	BMC
Hudaloff	24 Selected Compositions	Pro Art
Humperdinck-Carruthers	Evening Prayer	BMC
Isaac	Melody Book for Strings	CF
Kreuz	Gavotte, op. 13b, no. 8	Augener
Kreuz	The Violist, op. 13, Book 2	Augener
Lesinsky (ed)	34 Viola Solos (continue)	
Lovell	Four Country Sketches	Galaxy
Maganini	An Ancient Greek Melody	Ed M
Maganini	Song of a Chinese Fisherman	Ed M
Moffat-Palaschko	Alte Meister für junge Spieler	Schott
Mozart-Carruthers	Ländler	BMC
Murray and Tate	The New Viola Books, Book 2	Oxford
Pasfield	Three Simple Pieces	Mills
Roland-Fletcher	First Perpetual Motion	Mills
Schlemüller	A Song, op. 12, no. 1	CF
Schlemüller	Our Soldiers, op. 12, no. 5	CF
Schubert	The Fishermaiden	Augener
Schumann	Humming Song-Hunting Song, op. 68, no. 7	Augener
Streabborg-Applebaum	Waves at Play, op. 63	Belwin
Viguerie-Applebaum	Sonatina in C	Belwin
Whistler	Solos for Strings	Rubank
Wray	A Simple Suite	Oxford

Grade Three

Consolidate third position technic and introduce second, fourth, and fifth position. Playing in all positions up to fifth by rote. Reading in various positions may confuse the student. Begin instruction in vibrato if intonation development permits. Emphasize mixed bowings.

Example 9

RIGAUDON   Rameau-Applebaum

Example 10

STUDENT CONCERTO no. 2, op. 13   Seitz-Lifschey

Used by permission of G. Schirmer, Inc.

STUDY MATERIAL

Applebaum	Orchestral Bowing Etudes	Belwin
Applebaum	String Builder, Book 3	Belwin
Applebaum	Third and Fifth Position String Builder	Belwin
Best	Early String Shifting	Varitone
Carse	Viola School, Book 3, Progressive Studies	Augener
Fischer	Selected Studies and Etudes (First Position)	Belwin
Hofmann	First Studies, op. 86	International
Kayser	36 Studies, op. 43	International
Kayser-Vieland	36 Studies, op. 20	International
Lifschey	Scale and Arpeggio Studies, Book 1, In First Position	GS
Ševčik-Lifschey	Selected Studies in the First Position	GS
Whistler	From Violin to Viola	Rubank
Whistler	Introducing the Positions, Vol. I	Rubank
Wohlfahrt-Isaac-Lewis	Thirty Studies in First Position, op. 45, 54, 74	CF
Wohlfahrt-Vieland	30 Studies, op. 45 (continue)	

REPERTORY

J. S. Bach	Sheep May Safely Graze	Oxford
Bakaleinokoff	Air	BH
Bakaleinokoff	Gavotte	BH
Bakaleinokoff	Minuetto	BH
Bohm	Perpetual Motion no. 6 from Third Suite	CF
Boyce-Forbes-Craxton	Tempo di Gavotta	Oxford
Butterworth	Two French Pieces	Chappell
Chausson-Katims	Interlude	International
De Biase	Reverie	CF
Drigo-Ambrosio-Schloming	Serenade	CF
Dvořák	Humoresque, op. 101, no. 7	CF
Eckard (arr)	Highlights of Familiar Music	Presser

Fibich-Isaac-Lewis	Arioso	CF
Fitzenhagen	Cavatina, op. 39, no. 1	Augener
Forbes	First Year Classical Album	Oxford
Forbes (ed)	Second Year Classical Album	Oxford
Herfurth-deVeritch (ed)	Viola and Piano, A Collection	Willis
Handel	Sonata	Augener
Hook-Applebaum	Sonatina	Belwin
Isaac-Lewis (ed)	Londonderry Air	CF
MacDowell-Isaac	To a Wild Rose	CF
Mascagni-Deery	Siciliano	CF
Massenet-Deery	Melodie	CF
Mendelssohn	Song Without Words, op. 38, no. 2	Augener
Mendelssohn	Song Without Words, op. 53, no. 4	Augener
Mozart-Forbes	Minuet in C	Schott
Mozart-Radmall	Minuet and Trio	Chester
Mozart-Elkan	Sonatina in C	EV
Murray-Tate	The New Viola Books, Book 3	Oxford
Murrill	Four French Nursery Songs	Chester
Purcell-Forbes-Richardson	Sonata in G Minor	Oxford
Rameau-Applebaum	Rigaudon	Belwin
Saint-Saëns	Le Cygne	CF
Schmitt-Applebaum	Spring Song	Belwin
Schubert	Serenade	Augener
Schumann	Träumerei	CF
Seitz-Lifschey	Student Concerto, no. 2, op. 13	AMP
Tchaikowsky	Chanson Triste, op. 40, no. 2	CF
Tchaikowsky-Deery	None But the Lonely Heart	CF
Thomas-Isaac-Lewis	Gavotte from Mignon	CF
Wagner-Isaac-Lewis	Song to the Evening Star	CF

Intermediate Level

Grades four, five, and six, corresponding to the senior high school years, offer dozens of Baroque sonatas, numerous albums of pieces, and important concertos by Druschetzky, Handoshkin, Hoffmeister, Pleyel, Rolla, and Steiner, to mention a few. The Hoffmeister and Pleyel concertos, which are in the classical mold, help fill a conspicuous void. The Handoshkin concerto provides an excellent introduction to easy double-stops, while the Telemann-Rood *12 Fantasias* is a valuable aid in the development of the "Baroque style" of playing.

Grade Four

Emphasize the recognition of melodic and rhythmic patterns as an aid to more fluent music reading and improved technic. Introduce chromatic writing.

Increase emphasis on martelé and related bowings and on tonal development generally. Three-octave major and minor scales: C, D, E♭, E.

Example 11

FOURTH PUPIL'S CONCERTO
Seitz-Carruthers

Example 12

THE LEA RIG
arr. Forbes-Richardson

STUDY MATERIAL

Applebaum	Second and Fourth Position String Builder	Belwin
Bornoff	Patterns in Position	CF
Carse	Viola School, Book 4	Augener
Hofmann	15 Studies, op. 87 (largely first position, but difficult)	International
Kayser-Lesinsky	36 Elementary and Progressive Studies, op. 20	CF
Kayser	36 Studies, op. 43 (continue)	
Kreuz	Progressive Studies, Book 2, 3. Book 2 is in the flat keys, major and minor; Book 3 is in the sharp keys, major and minor	Augener
Kreuz	Select Studies for the Viola, Book 2	Augener
Lifschey	Scale and Arpeggio Studies, Book 2. In all positions	GS
Spaulding	Viola for Violinists	Varitone
Volmer	Studies	Schott
Whistler	Introducing the Positions, Vol. 2	Rubank
Wohlfahrt	30 Studies, op. 45 (continue)	
Wohlfahrt-Isaac-Lewis	30 Studies in First Position, op. 45, 54, 74 (continue)	

REPERTORY

J. S. Bach-Isaac	Arioso	CF
W. F. Bach-Altemark-Vieland	Three Duets for two violas	International
Beethoven-Forbes-Richardson	Country Dances	Oxford
Beethoven-Forbes	Rondo	Schott
Berger (ed)	Three 14th-Century Dances	MCA
Boetze (ed)	Viola Music for Concert and Church	BMC
Bornoff	The Violin Sings for viola solo with string orchestra or piano	CF
Corelli-Akon	Prelude and Allemande	Mills
Cui-Gottlieb	Orientale	CF
Delius	Serenade, from Hassan	BH
Doktor (ed)	Solos for the Viola Player	GS
Dyer	Three Pieces	Mills
Fibich-Isaac-Lewis	Poem	CF
Forbes (ed)	A Book of Classical Pieces	Oxford
Forbes (ed)	A Second Book of Classical Pieces	Oxford
Forbes and Richardson (arr)	Two Scottish Tunes	Oxford
Godard-Isaac-Lewis	Berceuse, from Jocelyn	CF
Goltermann-Isaac-Lewis	Andante, op. 14 (from Cello Concerto in A)	CF
Järnefelt	Berceuse	CF
Klengel	Album of Classical Pieces, 3 vol.	International
Klengel	Sonata in D	Ed M
Matz	Mixolydian Sonatina	Peters
Moore	Scottish Songs	Oxford
Pearson	Two Carols	Hinrichsen
Ponce-Isaac-Lewis	Estrellita	CF
Reed	Poem in G flat	CF
Rimsky-Korsakov	Song of India	CF
Schubert-Forbes	Reverie (from Piano Sonata in A, op. 120)	Oxford
Schubert-Piatigorsky	Adagio	EV
Schumann-Tobani	Serenade (the Voices of Love)	CF
Seitz-Carruthers	Fourth Pupil's Concerto	BMC
Seitz-Lifschey	Student Concerto no. 2 (First position)	AMP
Seitz-Klotman	Student Concerto (First movement from no. 5 in D)	Mills
Shield-Anderson	Tempo di Menuetto	Oxford
Sitt	Album Leaves, op. 39	International
Stravinsky-Forst	Berceuse (from The Fire-Bird)	Ed M
Telemann-Bergman-Forbes	Suite in D	AMP
Whistler and Hummel (ed)	Concert and Contest Album	Rubank

Grade Five

Continue study of the higher positions. Introduction of double-stops, chromatic scales, and all three-octave major scales. Use of martelé and sautillé bowing in scale playing. Special attention to velocity. One-octave scales on one string.

Example 13

TOCCATA   Paradies-Forbes

Example 14

THREE MINUETS   Schubert-Piatigorsky-Elkan

STUDY MATERIAL

Bruni	25 Melodious and Characteristic Studies	CF
		International
Carse	Viola School, Book 5	Augener
Dont-Svecenski	20 Progressive Exercises (second viola	
	accompaniment)	GS
Hofmann	15 Studies, op. 87	International
Hoffmeister-Hermann	12 Studies	International
Kayser-Lesinsky	36 Elementary and Progressive Studies,	
	op. 20 (continue)	
Kayser	36 Studies (continue)	
Kreuz	Progressive Studies, Book 4	Augener
Lifschey	Scale and Arpeggio Studies, Book 2	
	(continue)	

Ševčik-Tertis	School of Bowing Technic, op. 2, Part 1	Bosworth
Volmer	Studies (continue)	
Whistler	Introducing the Positions, Vol. 2 (continue)	
Wohlfahrt-Vieland	30 Studies, op. 45	International

REPERTORY

Accolay-Doty	Concerto no. 1	GS
Albeniz-Forbes	Tango	Oxford
J. S. Bach	Air, from Suite in D	Augener
J. S. Bach-Forbes-Richardson	Come, Redeemer of Our Race	Oxford
Beethoven-Forbes	Rondo	Oxford
Boetze (ed)	Viola Music for Concert and Church (continue)	
Boyce-Forbes-Craxton	Tempo di Gavotta	Oxford
Borissovsky-Conus-Katims	Album of Six Pieces	International
Couperin-Forbes-Richardson	Suite, From Concerts Royaux	Oxford
Debussy-Gretchaninoff-Katims	Beau Soir	International
Debussy-Cazden	Clair de Lune	Spratt
Debussy-Katims	Romance	International
Druschetzky	Concerto in D	Simrock
Doktor (ed)	Solos for the Viola Player (continue)	
Flackton	Sonata in G	Doblinger, Schott
Forsythe	Chanson Celtique	AMP
J. Haydn	Divertimento	EV
M. Haydn	Four Duos for violin and viola	OBV
Jacobson	Berceuse	Oxford
Jacobson	Three Varieties, a Suite for Three Violas	Mills
Kalliwoda-Vieland	Nocturnes, op. 186	International
Klengel (ed)	Classical Pieces	Peters
Liszt-Temesváry	Romance Oubliée	Kultura
Mozart-Courte	Divertimento in F	UMP
Mozart-Courte	Sonata in E flat	UMP
Paradies-Forbes	Toccata	Oxford
Saint-Saëns-Tertis	Melody	GS
Schubert-Elkan	Three Minuets	EV
Senaille-Katims	Allegro Spiritoso	International
Telemann	Concerto in G	International
Telemann-Schulz-Vieland	Sonata in A	International
Ticciati-Copperwheat	Scherzo and Toccata	Oxford

Valensin-Katims	Minuet	International
Vivaldi-Dallapiccola- Primrose	*Concerto in E Minor	International
Vivaldi-Dallapiccola- Primrose	6 Sonatas	International

*Also published as Sonata in E Minor in collection of 6 Sonatas listed above.

Grade Six

Continue the development of technic and tone. Use a bowing study for development of the lifted strokes, sautillé, and flying staccato. Add all three-octave minor scales.

Example 15

CONCERTO IN D   Hoffmeister

Example 16

LITANY FOR ALL-SOULS DAY   Schubert-Primrose

STUDY MATERIAL

Blumenstengel-Wiemann	24 Studies, op. 33	International
Bruni	25 Studies (continue)	
Hoffmeister-Hermann	12 Studies (continue)	
Kreuz	Select Studies, Book 3	Augener
Lifschey	Scale and Arpeggio Studies, Book 2: In all Positions (continue)	
Mazas-Pagels	Études Brilliantes, op. 36	International
Mazas-Pagels	Études Spéciales, op. 36	International
Palaschko	20 Studies, op. 36	International
Schradieck-Pagels	School of Viola Technique, Vol. 1	International

Ševčik-Tertis	Change of Position, op. 8	Bosworth
Sitt-Ambrosio	Practical Viola Method	CF
Volmer	Studies (continue)	

REPERTORY

C. P. E. Bach-Piccioli-Primrose	Sonata in G	International
J. S. Bach-Ries	Air and Gavotte	Schott
J. S. Bach-Pagels	Celebrated Air	CF
J. S. Bach	20 Preludes	Augener
J. S. Bach-	6 Suites for viola alone	

See page 114 for listing of nine editions

Clarke	Passacaglia	GS
Collet-Neuberth	Rhapsodie Castillane	Senart
Corelli-Akon	Prelude and Allemande	Mills
Corelli-Forbes-Richardson	Sonata da Camera	Oxford
Cowell	Hymn and Fuguing Tune no. 7	Peer
Creston	Homage	GS
Dittersdorf-Primrose	Andantino	International
Eccles	Sonata in G Minor	Peters
Fauré	Après un rêve	International
Fuleihan	Recitative and Sicilienne	GS
Galuppi-Tertis	Aria Amoroso	Augener
Granados-Katims	Orientale, Spanish Dance no. 2	International
Hampe	7 Short Baroque Dances	RE
Handel-Forbes-Richardson	Sonata in A, op. 1, no. 15	Oxford
Handel-Katims	Sonata in G Minor	International
Handoshkin-Vieland	Concerto	International
M. Haydn-Bonelli	4 Sonatas for violin and viola	Doblinger
Hoffmeister-Vieux	Concerto in D	Eschig
Jacob	Air and Dance	Oxford
Marais-Aldis-Rowe	Five Old French Dances	Chester
Marcello-Katims	Two Sonatas in G Minor and F	International
Mozart-Fuchs	Concerto, K. 216	MPH
Mussorgsky-Borissovsky	Hopak	International
Piston	Interlude	BH
Pleyel	Concerto in D	Peters
Pleyel	Duo for violin and viola, op. 44	Augener
Raff	Cavatina	CF
Ravel-Drouet	Pavane	Eschig
Richardson	Autumn Sketches	Oxford
Rivier	Concertino	Salabert
Rolla-Beck	Concerto	FC
Rolla-Rikko	3 Duets, for two violas	Mercury

Schoen	Six Easy and Melodic Duettinos for violin and viola	CF
Schubert-Primrose	Litany for All Souls Day	Schott
Schubert-Forbes	Sonata Movement	Augener
Schubert-Forbes	3 Sonatinas	Augener
Schubert-Ritter	Sonatina no. 1 in D	International
Schumann	Märchenbilder, op. 113	GS, BRH, Peters
Scriabin-Krane	Etude, op. 2, no. 1	GS
Seitz-Lifschey	Student Concerto no. 3, op. 12	AMP
Stamitz	3 Duets for two violas	Schott
Stamitz	6 Duos for violin and viola, op. 18	Leuckart
Steiner-Vieland	Concerto in D Minor, op. 43	International
Telemann-Rood	12 Fantasias for viola alone	MM
Telemann-Upmeyer-Vieland	Sonata in D	International
Telemann-Aspiazu	Sonata in E Minor for viola and guitar	ZM
Veracini-Katims	Largo	International
Vivaldi-Dallapiccola-Primrose	Sonatas (continue)	
Winkler	Meditation Elegiaque	Belaieff
Winkler	La Toupie	Balaieff

Advanced Level

The bulk of the viola literature falls into the advanced level of study, grades seven through ten, or the college years. Teachers who overlook the major works for viola do the student a grave injustice and deprive concert goers of a rewarding experience. Highly recommended are the viola works of Bartók, Bax, Benjamin, Bloch, Hindemith, Hovhaness, Milhaud, Partos, Piston, Schulman, Vaughan Williams, and Walton, among others. So numerous are the works in this advanced classification that exceptional works may be overlooked. The Walton Concerto, for example, was omitted from the American String Teachers Association's *String Syllabus*.

Grade Seven

Continue as before. Include scales in thirds, sixths, and octaves.

Example 17

FIRST ETUDE   Vieux

Example 18

CONCERTO IN B MINOR   Handel-Casadesus

Used by permission of G. Schirmer, Inc.

STUDY MATERIAL

Blumenstengel-Wiemann	24 Studies, op. 33 (continue)	
Campagnoli-Primrose	41 Caprices, op. 22	International
Dancla-Vieland	School of Mechanism, op. 74	International
Flesch-Karman	Scale System	CF
Hoffmeister-Hermann	12 Studies (continue)	
Kreutzer-Pagels	42 Studies	International
Kreuz	Scales and Arpeggios, Book 2	Augener
Kreuz	Select Studies, Book 4	Galaxy
Mazas-Pagels	Études Brilliantes, op. 36 (continue)	
Mazas-Pagels	Études Spéciales, op. 36 (continue)	International
Palaschko	20 Studies, op. 36 (continue)	
Primrose	The Art and Practice of Scale Playing on the Viola	Mills
Schradieck-Pagels	School of Viola Technique (continue)	

REPERTORY

J. C. Bach-Casadesus	Concerto in C Minor	Salabert
J. S. Bach-Ronchini	Andante (from the Italian Concerto)	Eschig
J. S. Bach-Forbes-Richardson	Prelude and Gavotte in A	Oxford
J. S. Bach	3 Sonatas	BRH, International, Peters, Ricordi
Beethoven-Forbes	Alla Polacca	Oxford
Beethoven-Forbes	7 Mozart Variations	Peters
Beethoven	Notturno, op. 42	GS, Schott
Beethoven-Tertis	Variations on a Theme of Mozart	BH
Bruch	Romanze	Eschig
Corelli-Katims	Sonata in D Minor	International
David	Concerto	Kultura
Dittersdorf-Lebermann	Concerto in F	Schott

Dittersdorf	Sonata in E flat	BRH, Hofmeister International
Dittersdorf	Symphonia Concertante for viola and double-bass	International
Eichner	Six Duets for violin and viola, op. 10	Nagels
Gibbs	Lyric Fantasy	Fox
Glazunov-Vieland	Elegy, op. 44	International
Handel-Casadesus	Concerto in B Minor	AMP, Eschig
Harrison	Lament	Galliard
Hovhaness	Talin Concerto	AMP
Hummel-Doktor	Sonata in E flat, op. 5, no. 3	Doblinger
Juon-Katims	Sonata in D, op. 16	International
Kabalevsky	Improvisation	MCA
Locatelli-Diktor	Sonata in G Minor	International
Marcello-Marchet	Sonata in E Minor	International
Milhaud	Sonata no. 1	Heugel
Moór-Katims	Prelude, op. 123	International
Nardini-Alard-Dessauer-Vieland	Sonata no. 1 in B flat	International
Nardini-Katims	Sonata in D	International
Paganini	Terzetto Concertante for viola, violoncello, and guitar	ZM
Polo	Studi-Sonate	MCA
Porpora-Alard-Dessauer	Sonata in E	International
Porter	Speed Etude	Valley
Porter	Suite for viola alone	Valley
Schumann	Adagio and Allegro	International
Schulman	Homage to Eric Satie	GS
Schulman	Theme and Variations	Chappell
Sitt-Vieland	Concertpiece in G Minor, op. 46	International
Skryabin-Borissovsky	Prelude in C sharp Minor	International
Stamitz	Three Duets for two violas	Schott
Stamitz-Primrose	Sonata in B flat	International
Tchaikowsky-Borissovsky	Nocturne in D Minor, op. 19, no. 4	International
Telemann-Dolmetsch	Sonata in A	AMP
Vaughan-Williams	Suite	Oxford
Vieux	Étude de Concert, no. 1 in C	Eschig
Vieux	Étude de Concert, no. 4 in F	Eschig
Vivaldi-Courte	Concerto in E	CF
Ward	Arioso and Tarantelle	Galaxy

Grade Eight

Use of advanced shifting studies and bowing variations. Review of all major and minor scales. Emphasis on the memorization and interpretation of multiple movement works from the literature.

Example 19

SONATA   Bax

Example 20

CONCERTO IN D   Stamitz

STUDY MATERIAL

Campagnoli-Primrose	41 Caprices, op. 22 (continue)	
Fiorello-Pagels	31 Studies	International
Fuchs	16 Fantasy Etudes	Ricordi
Hermann	Concert Studies, op. 18	International
Kreutzer-Pagels	42 Caprices (continue)	
Lukacs	Exercises in Change of Position	BH
Palaschko	Dedici Studii, op. 62	Ricordi
Rode-Pagels	24 Caprices	International
Rovelli-Pagels	12 Caprices, op. 3 and 5	International
Schradieck-Pagels	School of Viola Technique (continue)	

REPERTORY

Aguirre-Heifetz-Primrose	Huella	CF
C. P. E. Bach-Primrose	Solfegietto	CF
J. S. Bach	Three Sonatas (continue)	
Barnett-Primrose	Ballade, op. 16	Oxford
Bax	Sonata	Chappell
Beethoven-Vieland	Two Romances, op. 40 and 50	International

Bergsma	Fantastic Variations (on a theme from Tristan)	Galaxy
Boccherini-Sabatini	Sonata in C Minor	Mills
Brahms	Sonatas, op. 120	Peters
Brahms	2 Songs, op. 91 for also, viola and piano	Peters, Simrock
Clarke	Passacaglia	GS
Fuchs	Sonata Pastorale	AMP
Fuleihan	Recitative and Sicilienne	GS
Hindemith	Meditation	Schott
Krol	Lassus-Variationen, op. 33	Simrock
Leclair-Daniel	Sonata, "Le Tombeau"	International
Mozart-Forbes-Richardson	Adagio and Rondo	Oxford
Mozart	2 Duets for violin and viola	BRH, G.S., International, Peters, UE
Porpora-David-Hermann	Sonata in G	International
Porter	Duo for Viola and Harp (or harpsichord)	AMP
Reger	3 Suites, op. 131d for viola alone	International
Rolla	Escerzio ed Arpeggio	EdM
Stamitz	Concerto in D, op. 1	International
Tartini-Forbes-Richardson	Sonata in C, op. 1, no. 10	Oxford
Tartini-David-Hermann	Sonata in D	International
Tartini-Alard-Dessauer	Sonata no. 2 in F	International
Vale-Heifetz-Primrose	Ao pé da fogueira (Preludio XV)	CF
Veracini-Hermann-Vieland	Sonata in E Minor	International
Vieux	Étude de Concert no. 2	Eschig
Vieux	Étude de Concert no. 3	Eschig
Weber-Primrose	Andante e Rondo Ongarese	International

Grade Nine

Continue as before.

Example 21

CAPRICE   Brown

Example 22

FROM SAN DOMINGO   Benjamin

STUDY MATERIAL

Dont-Spindler	Studies, op. 35	Hofmeister
Dounis	Special Technical Exercises for Viola, op. 125	CF
Kreuz	Select Studies, Book 5	Augener
Rovelli-Pagels	12 Caprices, op. 3 and 5 (continue)	

REPERTORY

J. S. Bach-Kodaly	Fantasia Cromatica	BH
W. F. Bach-Pessl	Sonata in C	Oxford
Beethoven	Duet Eyeglasses Obbligato for viola and violoncello	International
Benjamin	From San Domingo	BH
Benjamin	Jamaican Rumba	BH
Berlioz-Liszt-Riley	Harold in Italy	UMP
Bloch	Meditation and Processional	GS
Bloch	Suite	GS
Boccherini-Katims	Sonata no. 6 in A	International
Borodin-Primrose	Nocturne (from String Quartet, no. 2)	Oxford
Borodin-Primrose	Scherzo (from String Quartet, no. 2)	Oxford
Brahms-Primrose	Wie Melodien zieht es mir, op. 105, no. 1	CF
Britten	Lachrymae	BH
Brown	Caprice	Salabert
Chopin-Sarasate-Rehfeld	Nocturne, op. 9, no. 2	CF
Clemens (ed)	Alte Meister des Violaspiels	Peters
Edmunds	Four Pieces	Mil
Enesco	Concertpiece	International
Freed	Rhapsody	CF
Harris	Soliloquy and Dance	GS

Hindemith	Sonata, op. 11, no. 4	Schott
Hoddinott	Concertino	Oxford
Jacoby	Fantasy	CF
Leighton	Fantasia on the name BACH	Novello
Milhaud	Quatre Visages	Heugel
Mozart-Stolz	Concerto in A flat	Soc
Mozart	Andante, Minuet and Rondo	BRH
Mozart	Sinfonia Concertante for violin and viola	Augener, BRH, Broude, GS, GT, Kalmus
Novacek-Ginot	Mouvement perpétuel	Jobert
Paganini-Vieland	Moto Perpetuo	International
Partos	Yiskor	MCA
Piston	Concerto	AMP
Porter	Duo for violin and viola	Valley
Rawsthorne	Sonata	Oxford
Reger	Three Suites, op. 131 D for viola alone (continue)	
Richter	Aria and Toccata	Mills
Russoto	Poem	MPH
Schubert-Katims	Sonata in A (Arpeggione)	International
Steiner	Rhapsodic Poem	MZK
Szekely	Rapsodia	Kultura
Vaughan-Williams-Shore	Romance	Oxford
Vieux	Étude de concert no. 3 in G	Eschig

Grade Ten

Example 23

SONATA, op. 11, no. 5   Hindemith

Das Thema sehr gehalten

Example 24

DER SCHWANENDREHER   Hindemith

Example 24 (Cont'd.)

STUDY MATERIAL

Gaviniès	24 Studies	International
Green	12 Modern Etudes for the Advanced Violist	EV
Paganini-Raby	24 Caprices, op. 1	International
Strauss-Steiner	Orchestral Studies	Peters

REPERTORY

J. S. Bach	Sixth Suite (from Cello Suites)	
Bartók	Concerto	BH
Bassett	Sonata, 1956	CFE
Bax	Fantasy	Chappell
Benjamin	Le Tombeau de Ravel	BH
Benjamin	Sonata or Concerto, Elegy, Waltz and Toccata	BH
Bliss	Sonata, 1934	Oxford
Bloch	Suite Hebraique	GS
Colgrass	Variations for 4 drums and viola	M Per
Corelli-Stoltz	Sonata No. 4 in B flat	Soc
Creston	Suite	Templeton
Dinicu-Heifetz	Hora Staccato	CF
Fricker	Concerto, op. 18	Schott
Hamilton	Sonata	Schott
Hindemith	Der Schwanendreher	Schott
Hindemith	Sonata op. 11, no. 5 for viola solo	Schott
Hoddinott	Concertino	Oxford
Holst	Lyric Movement	Oxford
Krenek	Sonata for viola solo	Bomart
Partos	Sinfonia Concertante	IMP
Persichetti	Infanta Marina, op. 83	EV
Riegger	Variations for violin and viola	AMP
Rubbra	Concerto	Lengnick
Serly	Concerto	MCA
Tartini-Radmall	Adagio and Fugue	Chester
Toch	Divertimento, op. 37, no. 2	Schott
Walton	Concerto	Oxford

32

REPRESENTATIVE PROGRAMS FOR ADVANCED PLAYERS

Over the years critical remarks concerning viola recitals have been directed toward the programming of too many transcriptions and the tendency among performers to retreat behind a big, voluminous tone, omitting musicianship and the need for dramatic contrast. Both criticisms are valid and can be avoided. Original music for viola exists in quantity and offers an enormous variety of styles. Subtlety of expression can be developed along with tone projection.

Ten representative recital programs that have been tested in public and have met with unusual success are listed below, merely as a point of departure. An additional ten programs could be designed by the imaginative violist.

I

Prelude from Suite VI	J. S. Bach
Sonata in C Minor	W. F. Bach-Pessl
Le Tombeau de Ravel (Valse Caprices)	Benjamin
Sonata in E flat, op. 120, no. 2	Brahms

II

Sonata da Camera	Locatelli
Notturno	Beethoven
Meditation from Nobilissima Visione	Hindemith
Sonata	Etler

III

Prelude	Moór
Sonata	Bax
Concertette	Gould
La Campanella	Paganini

IV

Concerto in B Minor	Telemann
Inventions (1962)	Lazarof
Divertimento	Dahl
Arpeggione Sonata	Schubert

V

Concerto in B Minor	Handel
Lachrymae, op. 48	Britten
Suite for viola alone	Porter
Märchenbilder, op. 113	Schumann

VI

Sonata in G Minor   Locatelli
Infanta Marina   Persichetti
Speed Etude   Porter
Suite   Vaughan Williams

VII

Chaconne for viola alone   K. P. E. Bach
Suite in D   Marais
Sonata, op. 11, no. 4   Hindemith
Suite Hebraique   Bloch

VIII

Gamba Sonata no 3 in G Minor   J. S. Bach
Sonata in E flat   Mozart
Nocturne   Borodin
Scherzo   Borodin
Concertstück   Enesco

IX

Sonata in E flat   Dittersdorf
Sonata no. 1   Milhaud
Five Old French Dances   Marais
Concerto   Bartók

X

Sonata in f, op. 120, no. 1   Brahms
Sonata (1942)   Benjamin
Suite   Bloch

FOREIGN TERMS USED IN VIOLA MUSIC

Foreign musical terms appear in even the most elementary viola music and should be learned for full comprehension of the score. The terms listed here are commonly found in solo viola music and represent a minimum list to serve as a point of departure. Each year of viola study should lead to an increase in vocabulary which will come about primarily as a result of the teacher's initiative. This list is intended as a convenient guide for the selection of terms to be incorporated in theory instruction on a year-by-year basis. A complete listing of all musical terms must be sought elsewhere.

A, Alla, All' — To, according.

A bene placito — Freely, at will.

Accelerando — Becoming faster.

Accento — Accented, stressed.

Accompagnato — Accompanied.

Accordatura — The pitch to which strings are normally tuned. The opposite of scordatura.

A due — In two parts. Play "divisi."

Affetto Affettuoso — Tenderly, affectionately.

Affrettando — Increased speed.

Aggiustamente — Rhythmically exact.

Agitato — Excited.

Alcuna, Alcuno — Somewhat.

Al fine — To the end.

Alla breve — Cut time, quick duple.

Allargando — Getting broader, therefore slower.

Allegramente — Bright, happy.

Allentando — Slowing down.

All' ottava — At the octave (above or below).

All' unisono — In unison.

Amabile — Lovingly.

Amoroso — Lovingly, warmly

Ancora — Once more, still more.

Ancora più forte — Still louder.

Animando — Becoming animated.

Animato — Animated.

Aperto — Open, clear, broad.

A piacere — Freely, at will. The same as "ad libitum."

Appassionato — Impassioned.

A punta d'arco — With the point of the bow.

Arcato — Bowed.

Arco — Bow.

Armonici — Harmonics.

Arpeggiato — To strum the four strings from lowest to highest in the manner of a guitar.

Arpeggio, Arpeggiando — Bouncing bow stroke with each bounce on a different string.

Assai — Very, much.

A tempo — Return to normal tempo.

Attaca — Begin without pause, attack suddenly.

A una corda — Play on one string only. Indicated by Roman numerals, I for A string, II for D, III for G, IV for C.

Battuta — Beat. "A battuta," in strict time. "Senza battuta," without any regular beat.

Bemolle — Flat.

Ben, Bene — Well, much.

Bene placito — At one's pleasure.

Bravura — Courage, boldness.

Brio — Spirit.

Calando — Gradually diminishing.

Calmato — Calm.

Calore, caloroso — Warmth.

Cantabile — Singing.

Cappricioso — Capricious, whimisical.

Coda, codetta — Concluding section.

Col, colla, coll' — With the.

Coll' Arco — With the bow.

Colla parte — With the part(s).

Colla punta d'arco — With the point of the bow.

Colla Voce — With the voice.

Col legno — Strike the string with the stick of the bow.

Coll' ottava — At the octave.

Colpo d'arco — Stroke of the bow.

Come — As, like.

Come prima — As at first.

Come sopra — As above.

Commodo — Comfortable, easy, neither too fast nor too slow.

Con — With.

Con afetto — With tender emotion.

Con amore — Lovingly.

Con anima — With spirit.

Con brio — Vigorously.

Concertante — Eighteenth-century term for symphonies with one or more solo instruments.

Concertino — Diminutive of Concerto.

Concerto — A work for one or more solo instruments with instrumental accompaniment.

Con fuoco — With fire.

Con sordino — With the mute.

Con spirito — With spirit, lively.

Continuo — Bass part (harpsichord, cello, or organ).

Contra — Against.

Corda — String.

Corda, spora una — Play on one string only.

Crescendo — Increasing volume.

Da Capo (D.C.) — From the beginning.

Dal Segno (D.S.) — From the sign.

Deciso — Decisively.

Declamato — Declamatory.

Decrescendo — Decrease in volume.

Delicato — Delicate.

Di molto — Extremely. "Allegro di molto," extremely fast.

Divisi (div.) — Divided.

Dolce — Sweetly, softly.

Dolcissimo — Very sweet.

Dolente — Sorrowfully.

Dolore — Sorrow.

Doloroso — Sorrowful.

Dopo — After.

Doppio — Double.

Doppio movimento — Double speed.

Due — Two.

Due corde — Same tone sounded on two strings.

E, ed — And.

Equale — Equal.

Energico — With vigor, energetically.

Espressione — Expression, feeling.

Espressivo — Expressively.

Estinguendo — Dying away.

Facilmente — Lightly, easily.

Fermata — Pause, sustain.

Feroce — Fierce.

Fine — End, close.

Fino — As far as.

Flautando, flautato — Flutelike effect achieved by bowing lightly over the finger-board.

Forte (f) — Loud, strong.

Forte-piano (fp) — Loud, then immediately soft.

Fortissimo (ff) — Very loud.

Forza — Strength, vigor, force.

Forzando, forzato (fz) — Forced, accented.

Fuoco — Fire, force.

Furioso — Furious.

Giocoso — Playful, humorous.

Giusto — Appropriate. "Tempo Giusto" in strict tempo (non-rubato).

Glissando — Rapid scale-like passage produced by a series of minute movements of the left hand.

Gradatamente — Gradually.

Gran — Large, much.

Grandevole — Pleasant, pleasing.

Grandioso — In an imposing manner.

Grave — Grave, solemn.

Grazioso — Gracefully.

Gusto — Style, zest.

Incalzando — Pressing, hurrying.

Inciso — Incisive.

In modo di — In the manner of.

Inquieto — Restless, uneasy.

Istesso — Same. "L'istesso tempo," in the same time.

Lacrimoso — Mournful.

Lamentando, Lamentoso — Lamenting.

Lancio — Vigor.

Legato — Smoothly, connectedly.

Leggiero — Light, graceful.

Legno — Wood. "Col legno," to tap the strings with the stick of the bow.

Liberemente — Freely, at will.

Licenza, con alcuno — Indication for freedom or license in performance.

L'istesso tempo — The same tempo.

Lontanto — Distant.

Lungo — Long.

Ma — But.

Maestoso — Majestic.

Maggiore — Major.

Magno — Great.

Man, mano — Hand.

Marcato — Emphasized, stressed, marked.

Martellando, Martellato — Hammered. Detached strokes at the point of the bow.

Marziale — In the style of a march.

Meno — Less.

Meno mosso — Less quickly.

Mesto — Sad, mournful.

Mezza, Mezzo — Half, moderate.

Minore — Minor.

Misterioso — Mysterious.

Misura — Measure, meter.

Modo — Manner, style.

Molto — Very, much.

Mosso — Moved, lively. "Piu mosso," faster. "Meno mosso," slower.

Morendo — Dying.

Moto — Motion.

Movimento — Speed. "Lo stesso movimento," at the same speed.

Niente — Nothing.

Non — Not.

Nuovo — New.

O — Or.

Obbligato — An independent accompanying part.

Ondeggiando — Undulating tremolo indicated by a wavy line over repeated notes.

Ordinario – Ordinary, normal. "Modo ordinario," return to the normal way.

Ossia – Or, alternate.

Ottava – Octave.

Parte – Part, voice.

Per – By, in order to.

Perdendosi – Dying away.

Pesante – Heavy.

Piacevole – Agreeably.

Pieno – Full.

Più – More.

Più allegro – More quickly.

Piuttosto – Rather. "Andante piuttosto allegro," rather fast than slow.

Pizzicato – Plucked.

Placido – Calm, peaceful.

Pleno – Full.

Pochettino – Very little.

Poco – Little.

Poco a poco – Little by little.

Poi – Later, then.

Ponderoso – Heavy, ponderous.

Ponticello, sul – Bow near the bridge producing a glassy tone.

Portamento – Carried over, smooth. Sliding between two pitches without distinguishing the intermediate tones.

Portato – Somewhat detached.

Precipitando – Impetuously.

Preciso - Precise.

Pressante, Pressando – Urgent, hurrying.

Prima – First. "Prima volta," a first ending when a repeat is indicated.

Punta, punto – Point.

Quasi – As if, almost.

Quieto – Quiet, calm.

Rallentando – Becoming gradually slower.

Ravvivando – Quickening.

Replica – Repeat.

Resoluto – Resolutely.

Rinforzando (rf., rfz.,) – Reinforced.

Riprendere – Resume tempo.

Ripieno – Full orchestra.

Ripresa – Repeat, recapitulation.

Risoluto – Resolute, determined.

Risvegliato – In an animated manner.

Ritard, ritardando (rit., ritard.) – Slowing gradually.

Ritenuto (rit.) – Slowing immediately.

Ritmico – Rhythmically.

Rubato – Flexible tempo.

Saltato, saltando — Bouncing bow. A rapid spiccato.

Scala — Scale.

Scherzando — Playful, joking.

Sciolto — Free and easy.

Scordatura — Tune to indicated pitches, contrary to accordatura.

Secco — Dry.

Segno — Sign.

Segue — Follow without pause.

Semplice — Simply.

Sempre — Always, continuously.

Senza — Without.

Senza sordino — Take off the mute.

Sforzando, sforzato (sf, sfz) — Suddenly accented, forced.

Simile, simili — In a like manner.

Sinfonia — Symphony. Overture.

Sinfonia concertante — An orchestral work with one or more solo instruments.

Sinfonietta — A short symphony.

Slentando — Becoming gradually slower.

Smorzando — Dying away.

Sonare — To sound or play.

Sopra — Above.

Sordino — Mute. "Senza sordino," without the mute. "Via sordino," take off the mute.

Sostenuto — Sustained.

Sotto — Under, below.

Sotto Voce — In an undertone.

Spiccato — Clearly articulated. The bow is thrown on the string and rebounds or is lifted producing a very short tone.

Spirito — Spirit.

Spiritoso — Spirited.

Staccato — Detached, separated.

Stentando — Holding back each note. Laboring.

Steso — Slow.

Stesso — Same.

Stile — Style.

Strepitoso — Noisy.

Stretto — Quickening of pace.

Stringendo — Accelerating the tempo.

Su — On, near.

Subito — Suddenly.

Sul, sull, sulla — On, at.

Sul ponticello — Bow near the bridge producing a glassy tone.

Sul tasto, sulla tastiera — Bow lightly over the fingerboard.

Suono — Sound.

Tacet, tacent — Silent.

Tallone — Frog. "Al Tallone," at the frog.

Tanto — Much, so much.

Tastiera — Fingerboard. "Sulla tastiera, on the fingerboard.

Tardo — Slow, "Tardando," becoming slower.

Tedesca — German-like.

Tema — Theme, subject.

Tempo — Speed of the basic pulse.

Teneramente — Tenderly.

Tenuto — Sustained, held.

Tirato — Down-bow.

Tono — Key, mode, tone.

Tosto — Quick, Piu tosto, faster.

Tranquillo — Calm.

Trattenuto — Holding back with a sustained quality.

Tremolo, tremolando — Reiteration of the same tone by rapid alternation of the bow direction.

Tristo — Sad.

Troppo — Too much.

Tutti — All, everyone.

Un poco — A little.

Veloce — Fast.

Via — Away.

Vibrato — Minute fluctuations of pitch produced by oscillations of the left hand.

Vigore — Vigorous.

Viola — A generic term of the sixteenth century for any bowed string instrument. In modern usage, the alto (or tenor) member of the violin family.

Viola da braccio — "Arm viol." Refers collectively to members of the violin family.

Viola d'amore — A bowed string instrument of the seventeenth and eighteenth centuries the size of a treble viol. having sympathetic strings stretched below the bowed strings.

Vivace — Lively.

Voce — Voice.

Volti — Turn over (the page).

Vuota — Empty. "Corda vuota," open string.

FRENCH

À la, À l' — To the, at the.

Allègrement — Brightly, gaily.

Alto — Viola.

Animé — Animated.

Après — After.

Archet — Bow.

Arraché — Forceful pizzicato.

Assez — Somewhat, enough.

Au, Aus — To the, at the.

Au chevalet — Bow near the bridge producing a glassy tone.

Au-dessous — Beneath, less than.

Au mouvement — Normal speed.

Aussi — Also, as, therefore.

Au talon — Bow at the frog.

Autre — Other.

Avant — Before, forward.

Avec — With.

Balancement — Tremolo.

Bariolage — Changing strings rapidly, the higher tones being produced from the lower strings.

Beaucoup — Much, many.

Bémol — Flat.

Bien — Well, much, very.

Bis — Again, repeat.

Cédant — Slowing down.

Cédez — A slight holding back, poco ritardando.

Chantant — Singing.

Chevalet — Bridge.

Comme — Like, in the manner of.

Concertant — Eighteenth-century term for symphonies with one or more solo instruments.

Corde — String.

Coup d'archet — Bow stroke.

Dehors — Outside.

Dehors, en — Emphasized.

Démancher — Shifting of the left hand from one position to another.

Demi — Half.

Dessus — Above.

Détaché — Detached, separated.

Dièse — Sharp.

Diminuant — Diminish in loudness.

Double corde — Double stop.

Douce — Gentle, soft.

Doucement — Gently, smoothly.

Doux — Sweet.

Échelle — Scale.

École — School or method.

Égal — Equal.

Élan — Dash, impetuosity.

Élargir — To broaden. "Elargissant," broadening.

Emporte' — Excited.

En — In, while, as.

Enchaînez — Follow with no break, seque.

Encore — Again, repeat, still.

En dehors — Emphasized.

Et — And.

Étouffé — Muted.

Expressif — Expressive.

Fin — End.

Fois — Time.

Fort — Always.

Gamme — Scale.

Glisser — To slide.

Gracieux — Gracefully.

Gros — Great, large.

Harmonique — Harmonic.

Harmoniques, son — Play harmonics.

Haut — High.

Inquiet — Restless.

Jeu — Play. "Jeu ordinaire," play normally.

Jouer — To play.

Joyeux — Joyful.

Jusqu'à — Until. "Jusqu'à la fin," until the end.

Laisser — Permit, allow.

Large — Broad, slow and dignified.

Léger, légèremente — Light, lightly.

Libre, Librement — Freely, at will.

Lié — Bound, tied, slurred.

Lour, lourde — Heavy, "Lordeur," heaviness.

Mais — But.

Majeur — Major.

Marqué — Marked, emphasized.

Martelé — Hammered. Detached strokes at the point of the bow.

Même. — Same.

Mélodique — Melodic.

Mesure — Measure, meter.

Mettre — To put. "Mettez la Sourd," put on the mute.

Mineur — Minor.

Modére — Moderate speed.

Moins — Less.

Mouvement — Tempo, movement. "Au movement," in time.

Ne que — Only.

Ondulé — Undulating tremolo. An obsolete form of tremolo.

Ordinaire — Ordinary, normal.

Ôtez, ôter — Take off.

Ou — Or.

Parlando, parlante — Expressive declamation.

43

Pas — Not, not any.

Pathetique — Pathetic.

Petit — Small.

Peu — A little.

Peu à peu — Little by little.

Pincé — Pinched.

Plein — Full.

Plus — More.

Pour — For.

Poussé — Up-bow.

Poussez — Push ahead. Quicken the tempo.

Précipité — Impetuously.

Premier — First.

Pressez, Pressant — Urgent, hurrying.

Pupitre — A stand of players. A term indicating the dividing of parts.

Que — That, as.

Ralentir — Becoming gradually slower.

Renforcer — To reinforce.

Répétez — Repeat.

Reprendre — To take up again. "Reprenez le mouvement, "return to tempo.

Restez — Remain in one position. Do not shift position of the left hand.

Retenant, retenu — Holding back immediately, ritenuto.

Sans — Without.

Sautillé — Bouncing bow. A rapid spiccato.

Sec, sèche — Dry.

Serré — Pressing, getting quicker. "En serrant," accelerating the tempo.

Sombre — Melancholy, somber.

Sonore — Sonorous, with full tone.

Sour, sourdine — Mute. "Mettez la Sourd," put on the mute. "Otez les sourdines," take off the mutes.

Sous — Under.

Suivez — With the parts, follow.

Sur — On, over.

Sur la pont — Bow near the birdge.

Sur la touche — Bow lightly over the fingerboard.

Talon — Frog of the bow.

Tant — As much, much.

Timbre — Texture or quality of sound.

Tirer, tirez, tiré — Down-bow.

Ton — Tone, key, mode.

Touche — Fingerboard.

Tous, tout — All, everyone.

Très — Very much.

Triste — Sad.

Trop — Too much.

Un peu — A little.
Unis — Play together following divisi in orchestra music.
Ut — "C."
Varié — Varied.
Vif — Lively.
Vite, vitement — Fast, quickly.
Voix — Voice.

GERMAN

Ab — Off.
Abdämpfen — To mute.
Aber — But.
Abstrich — Down-bow.
Alle — All, everyone.
Allein — Alone, unaccompanied.
Allmählich — Gradually.
Am Frosch — Bow at the frog.
Am Griffbrett — Bow over the fingerboard.
Am Steg — Bow near the bridge producing a glassy tone.
Anfang — Beginning. "Vom Anfang," da capo, from the beginning.
Anhalten — Slowing down.
Anreissen — Forceful attack.
Anschwellend — Crescendo.
Auch — Also, but.
Auf — On, at, up.
Aufbewegt — Lively.
Aufhalten — Slowing down.
Aufstrich — Up-bow.
Aus — From, out of.
Ausdruck — Expression, feeling.
Ausdrucksvoll — With great feeling.
Be — Flat.
Bebend — Tremolo.
Bedächtig — Steady and unhurried.
Belebt — Brisk, animated.
Beruhig, beruhigend — Calm, quieting.
Beschleunigen — To speed up.
Bewegt — Animated, with motion. "Bewegter," animato.
Bis — Until.
Bogen — Bow.
Bombo — Eighteenth century term for tremolo.
Bratsche — Viola. An adaptation of the Italian "viola da braccio."
Bratschist — Violist.
Breit — Broad.

Breit gestrichen — Broadly bowed.

Dämpfer — Mute. "Mit Dämpfer," with mute. "Dämpfer weg," without mute. "Ohne Dämpfer," take off the mute.

Deutlich — Clearly, distinctly.

Doch — Yet, still.

Doppel — Double.

Doppelgriff — Double stop.

Drängend — Pressing on.

Dur — Major.

Durch — Through.

Eilend, mit Eile — Hurrying.

Einfach — Single, simple.

Empfindung — Feeling, emotion. "Empfindungsvoll," full of feeling.

Etwas — Somewhat, rather.

Flageolettöne — Harmonics.

Fliessend — Flowing. "Fliessender," more flowing.

Folgen — To follow.

Frei — With freedom.

Frisch — Brisk, lively, fresh.

Fröhlich — Joyful.

Gabelgriff — Cross fingering.

Gebrochene Dreiklänge — Arpeggios, broken chords.

Gebunden — Legato.

Gedämpft — Muted. "Nicht gedämpft," not muted.

Gehen — Going.

Gehend — Moving at a moderate speed, andante.

Gehalten — Held out, sustained.

Gekneipt — Plucked, pizzicato.

Gelassen — Quiet, calm.

Gemächlich — Comfortable, comodo.

Gemässigt — Moderate.

Geschlagen — Tap the string with the bow stick (col legno battuto).

Gestrichen — Draw the bow stick across the string (col legno).

Geteilt — Divided.

Getragen — Sustained, slow, sostenuto.

Gewichtig — Heavy, ponderous.

Gleich — Like, equal.

Gleichmässig — Even.

Gross — Great, large.

Gut — Good, well.

Harmonisch — Harmonic.

Halb, Halbe, Hälfte — Half.

Halt — Hold, pause. "Halten," to hold, sustain.

Haupt — Head, chief, main.

Hauptstimme — Principal part.

Hauptzeitmass — Tempo I.
Heftig — Violent.
Heiss — Hot, ardent.
Heiter — Cheerful.
Hell — Clear, bright.
Herabstrich, Herstrich, Herunterstrich — Down-bow.
Heraufstrich, Hinstrich — Up-bow.
Hinsterbend — Fading away.
Hoch — High, much.
Im — In the.
Immer — Always, ever, still.
Innig — Heartfelt, inward.
Klagend — Lamenting.
Klar — Clear, distinct.
Klein — Small
Komponiert — Composed, put-together.
Konzert — Concert, concerto.
Kräftig — Strong, vigorous.
Kurz — Short.
Lage — Position.
Lang — Long.
Langsam — Slow. "Langsamer," slower.
Lebhaft — Lively. "Lebhafter," livelier.
Leicht — Light, easy.
Leidenschaftlich — Passionate.
Leise — Soft, gentle. "Leiser," softer.
Leibesgeige — Viola d'Amore
Luftig — Airy, thin.
Lustig — Cheerful.
Mächtig — Powerful, mighty.
Mal — Time, occasion.
Markiert — Marked marcato.
Mässig — Moderate.
Mehr — More.
Melodisch — Melodic.
Mit — With.
Mitte — Middle.
Möglich — Possible.
Moll — Minor.
Munter — Lively.
Nach — After.
Nachdrücklich — Emphatic, expressive.
Nachlassend — Relaxing.
Nicht — Not.
Niederstrich — Down-bow.

Noch — Still, yet, even.
Nur — Only.
Ober — Over, upper
Oder — Or.
Ohne — Without.
Oktaven — Octaves.
Pause — Pause, rest.
Rasch — Quick.
Rauschend — Rustling, murmuring.
Ruhig — Calm, quiet.
Saite — String.
Satz — Movement.
Schleppen — To drag. "Nicht schleppen," do not drag.
Schnell — Fast.
Schwärmer — Eighteenth century term for tremolo.
Schwer — Heavy, difficult.
Schwindend — Dying away.
Schwungvoll — Animated, spirited.
Sehr — Very much.
Spielen — To play.
Spitze — Point. "An der spitze." At the point.
Springbogen — Bouncing bow.
Stark — Strong. "Starker," louder.
Steg — Bridge. "Am steg," bow near the bridge producing a glassy tone.
Stets — Steadily.
Still — Quiet, calm.
Stimme — A part.
Streich — Bow.
Strich — Bow stroke.
Stück — Piece, composition.
Stürmisch — Stormy, violent.
Teil — Part, section.
Tonleiter, tonarten, tonischen — Scales.
Träumerisch — Dreamy.
Traurig — Mournful, sad.
Über — Over, above.
Übung — Exercise, study.
Und — And.
Unruhig — Restless.
Unter- — Below, under.
Viel — Many, much.
Vollstimmig — Full-voiced.
Vom Anfang — From the beginning.
Vor — For.
Vortragen — To bring forward prominently.

Vorwarts – Forward, continue. "Vorwarts gehend," faster.
Warme – Warmth.
Weg – Away, off.
Wehmütig – Sad, melancholy.
Wenig – Little. "Weniger," less.
Werden – To become.
Wie – As, like, as if.
Wieder – Again.
Zählzeit – Beat.
Zart – Tender, delicate.
Zeitmass – Tempo, speed.
Ziemlich – Rather.
Zu – To, for.
Zum – To them, at the.
Zurück – Back again. "Zuruckgehend," going back (to the original tempo).
Zurückhalten – To hold back.
Zweimal – Twice.

Tempo Graduations–Slow to Fast

	Italian	French	German
Extremely slow	Larghissimo Lentissimo Adagissimo	Très lent	Sehr langsam Ganz langsam
Very slow	Largo Lento Adagio	Lent Large	Langsam Breit
Rather slow	Larghetto	Un peu lent	Etwas langsam
Slow, with motion	Andante Andantino	Allant Très modéré	Mässig langsam Gehend
Moderately	Moderate	Modéré	Mässig Mässig bewegt
Rather fast	Allegretto	Un peu animé	Etwas bewegt
Fast, quick	Allegro	Animé	Bewegt Schnell
Animated	Animato	Animé	Belebend Belebt
Very fast	Vivace Vivo Presto	Vif Vite	Lebhaft Eilig
Extremely fast	Prestissimo	Très vif	Ganz schnell Ganz lebhaft

Altmann, Wilhelm; and W. Borissowsky. *Literaturverzeichnis für Bratsche und Viola d'amore* (1937). Verlag für musikalische Kultur under Wissenschaft.

American String Teachers Association. *String Syllabus* (1963). ASTA.

Farish, Margaret. *String Music in Print* (1965). Bowker.

Farish, Margaret. *Supplement to String Music in Print* (1968). Bowker.

National Interscholastic Music Activities. *Selective Music Lists* (1967). MENC.

Rolland, Paul (Editor). *List of Contemporary String Music* (1959). ASTA.

Zeyringer, Franz. *Literatur für Viola* (1963). Hartberg.

Chapter II

MUSICAL ASPECTS OF TEACHING VIOLA

THE LESSON–THE PRACTICE PERIOD

In the last few decades, teaching methods have improved in every respect, particularly in the area of mental training. Where the stress had been on imitation and trial and error learning, teachers now emphasize the comprehension of principles and the efficient use of one's time. No longer are the lesson and the practice period viewed as separate entities. Having the same objective, improved performance, the two are similarly organized and serve as an extension of each other. Lessons are given over to an explanation and demonstration of the principles of playing, the accumulation of effective study and work habits, the diagnosis and solution of learning difficulties, and the setting of realistic, short-term goals, all of which carry over into the practice session. As analytical in intent as the lesson, the practice period accents quality rather than quantity of effort. Effective teaching, which is stimulating and challenging, leads to effective practice. The two are inseparable.

Instrumental study may be set up as a sequence of sub-tasks ordered in successive steps that builds a solid foundation for technical advancement. Such sequential analysis facilitates learning and prevents the skipping of essential steps. Although individual differences rule out exact prescriptions for teaching, a workable pattern may be presented as a guide to teachers seeking ideas to incorporate in their own unique situation.

A Workable Learning Sequence

1. Edit the music, writing-in suitable fingerings and bowings.
2. With the student, preview the contents of the music to be studied.
3. Point out those musical elements which are appropriate to the student's degree of advancement: keys, finger patterns, phrases, cadences, scale-line and arpeggiated passages, dynamics, rhythmical figures, bowing patterns, repetitions, sequences, modulations, transitional material, musical character, the development of ideas.
4. Ask the student questions that call for recognition, analysis, and evaluation. Inability to discuss music intelligently will be reflected in a corresponding

lack of thought during the practice period. A failure to recognize patterns indicates a need for theory training.

5. Point out the sections that are technically difficult and analyze the types of problems to be encountered.

6. Establish a goal that is readily attainable. Work out the correct movement patterns separating the left and right hands, if necessary. The breaking down of problems is a clear demonstration to the student of a correct practice approach. Do not introduce a new problem before the first goal has been attained.

7. Have the student play slowly, setting the correct sequence of muscular patterns before increasing speed. With repetition, movements become more refined and more automatic. As the student gains facility in a controlled situation, he also gains confidence in his ability to perform with accuracy. The solving of technical problems frees the player for attention to musical content.

8. Review for the retention of ideas. Specify precisely what the student is to accomplish before his next lesson and how he is to go about doing it.

The major goal of every teacher is to convince the student that mental involvement is necessary for successful performance. The use of rote teaching frees the younger student to concentrate on rhythmical patterns, tonal relationships, and problems in technique. Gymnastic drills of various types prepare and condition the student for performance. Rhythmical variations of scales and familiar melodies make excellent bowing studies during rote teaching.

A second goal of the teacher is to simplify problems in order that an easy solution may be found. Modern techniques used by successful teachers include the use of preliminary motions with and without the viola, as an aid to kinesthetic development. Left- and right-hand problems must be clearly separated. Frequently the reduction of difficult passages to open string equivalents allows full attention to be directed to difficulties in bowing as illustrated in Example 25.

Example 25

Concerto   Walton

Andante con moto, measures 59-62

Example 25 (Cont'd)

Alteration of note values forming various rhythms that place the accent first on one finger and then on another is a technique to develop facility, fluency and evenness in the left hand (Example 26).

Example 26

Sinfonia Concertante   Mozart

Allegro maestoso, measures 66-67

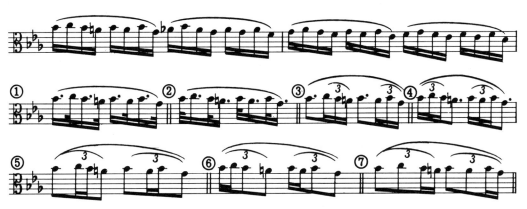

Many teachers introduce the use of staccato bowing early in instruction in order to develop a consciousness of bow division and security in balancing and controlling the bow. The early introduction of spiccato provides a sensory experience in controlling arm weight and the suspension of the bowing unit from the shoulder joint. Finally, the use of Suzuki's stop-think-play technique encourages the domination of physical activity by mental control, allowing the requisite time to set up motion patterns.

Organization of Practice Time

Students of all ages need help in organizing their practice time. Parents are prone to attribute poor practice to a lack of motivation and frequently do little in helping their children to arrange a workable schedule or to budget their time wisely. The use of a practice contract specifying what is expected of parent, student, and teacher delineates the role of each and assigns to the parent and student specific responsibilities which are often overlooked. Ideal practice conditions should include: a quiet, well-lighted, comfortable room in which to work; practice scheduled as soon as possible following lessons at a time when the student is better oriented to his material and his memory is still clear, requiring less review time; regular, spaced practice sessions of adequate length with breaks held to a minimum; practice scheduled early rather than late in the day.

Even with specific instructions as to the use of practice time, students tend to develop bad habits which must be ferreted out if progress is to continue. An understanding of poor practice patterns is essential in guiding the student toward a more efficient and profitable use of his time.

Patterns of Poor Practice to be Avoided

Playing through the entire assignment without concentration.
Thoughtless repetition reinforcing incorrect action patterns.
Wasteful repetition beyond the limit required to master the task.
Emphasizing technically easy material and avoiding problem areas.
Disregarding bowings and fingerings and failing to learn specific action patterns.
Playing too fast to hear mistakes or to effect corrections.
Practicing too slowly to acquire facility.
Pounding of fingers and accenting of bow resulting in an unmusical effect.
Overly analytical, pedantic practice to the extent that inner feeling is destroyed.

MUSIC READING

Viola teachers in the United States have identified music reading as the greatest problem encountered in changing over a student from violin to viola. While a large part of this difficulty stems from learning a new clef, the general ability to read music at sight is the mark of a well-trained musician and should receive a proper share of emphasis on the part of the teacher.

Reading music is a perceptual and a sensory process involving thinking, understanding, and hearing as well as seeing. To a degree, the ability to read music is subject to experience, opportunity, and maturity. Auditory, visual, kinesthetic, and motivational factors also play a large part in the process. Note recognition is but one of the required skills. The special music vocabulary, symbols of musical notation, and concepts of key relationships, with attendant complexities of finger patterns, pose particular problems for the student and require from the teacher extreme care in curriculum planning and in matching material to student level of achievement.

Readers experiencing difficulties have recognizable symptoms: uncertainty in performance, rhythmical unsteadiness, inability to recognize patterns, failure to see large units, and the use of too many eye fixations. If a student has accumulated poor reading habits, practice tends to reinforce them. The development of reading skill is strongly dependent on the teacher's ability to key material to the individual's intelligence, musicality, and performance ability and to emphasize music theory as a part of the lesson plan. Inexperienced readers need many opportunities to practice on easy, interesting music with the specific objective of improving speed in reading. Negative attitudes about reading fade away as more skill and confidence are acquired.

Gauge for Reading Level

Aside from drawing on material from graded lists, each teacher may derive his own readability formula to determine student level. This formula should reflect an evaluation of the following items:

> Rhythmical complexities (bowing)
> Tonal complexities (keys and finger patterns)
> Number of new problems introduced
> Extent of technical difficulties
> Total length
> Attractiveness of material to student
> Individual maturational deviations
> Local standards of achievement
> Teacher's own pedagogical methods

A breakdown in reading music may be traced to inadequacies in instrumental technique not directly associated with reading but indicating the need for easier material. Often the number or quality of prior experiences in reading is insufficient for the level of material to be read or the student has had insufficient training in music theory. The teacher should be alert to the possibility of deficiencies in vision or hearing or the presence of correlated defects such as motor incoordination, mixed dominance, or lefthandedness.

Improvement in reading may be accelerated by the teacher in several ways. Reading level may be set slightly below performing level and the reading speed adjusted to the level of difficulty of the music. The student should have many opportunities to read music at each grade level. Music theory and the problem of recognition of patterns should be emphasized at each lesson.

A knowledge of music fundamentals (meter, rhythm, dynamics, tempo, bowings, fingerings, etc.) and the recognition of musical devices (sequences, inversions, modulations, etc.) are essential parts of instruction that the teacher must not neglect. Every student should be trained to scan music to see what is there and encouraged to search for relationships. The use of theory work books and flash cards or other visual aids in a graded sequence as a planned part of instruction will provide the experience needed for ease in music reading and in learning the alto clef.

Many skills are called into play in performing from printed music. As the teacher guides the development of these special skills, an overall improvement in music reading takes place.

Concentration and personal discipline increase the ability to follow directions. The improvement of facility in performance, the goal of every lesson, quickens the reaction to the printed page. Proficiency in associating visual symbols with actual sounds and with their location on the instrument are basic skills the teacher should emphasize during early instruction. Finally, continual emphasis of music theory should improve the student's ability to remember melodies and his proficiency in executing rhythmic notation correctly.

Rhythmical Reading

Few students are able to comprehend the fractional arithmetic of music early in their study. The difficulty lies in music itself. At best our system of counting defies logic. The usual musical symbol for one beat is a quarter note while a whole note represents four beats. In counting we say "one" as the musical tone begins not as it ends as would be the case in any other type of measurement. Most music teachers identify note values in terms of beats as they appear in the measure, not in terms of the length of the notes themselves. The practice of counting beats does not develop a sense of timing. If anything this practice stresses addition and relates to what is past, not what is ahead.

Most students begin string study through a rote approach, moving rapidly into divisions of the quarter note into sixteenths to free the elbow joint. In very little time quite complex rhythms are covered, taking advantage of the student's aural ability to remember and recognize patterns. The natural impulse to begin music reading with these complex rhythms must be resisted. The eye needs considerable practice in spotting the basic quarter note beat before subdivision is attempted.

Often word similarities aid the recognition of rhythmic patterns involving subdivision. To young students ♪♪♪♪ ♪ ♪ may sound similar to "Watch me bend my el-bow" or "Don't forget to practice." ♪♪♪ becomes "fid-del-ing." ♪♪. is aided by "Quick change" or "Right on." Even unnatural rhythms such as ♪♪♪♪♪ encountered by more advanced students may be simplified by thinking "un-i-ver-si-ty" or "Lol-lo-bri-gi-da." With a large amount of imagination and a minimum of time, the teacher will be able to replace the addition of fractions and the hazards of the bar line with a system emphasizing continuous rhythmical flow that moves phrase-wise by important notes.

Etling, Forest	*Workbook for Strings,* Books 1 and 2	Etling
Janowsky, Edward	*Viola Note Speller*	Belwin
Martin, Pauline	*Keyway Theory Book*	Pro Art

The Alto Clef

Learning to read music involves the acquisition of a series of skills. Generally accepted as a first step in the series in string study is the identification of the location of notes representing open strings. Upon this foundation, new notes are added in a gradual, cumulative process. For students with previous musical training, a wise practice is to relate the alto clef with the more common soprano and bass clefs and with the tunings of neighboring stringed instruments.

Example 27

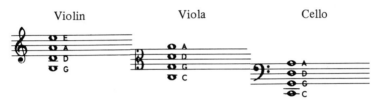

In transferring advanced students from violin to viola, pitch identification must not be overlooked. Devices and tricks employed to allow quick reading of the viola clef are questionable if they do not require identification of pitch names. Students who play viola for long periods without being made aware of pitch names make less progress than those students who effect a slower but more learned transfer.

The most common quick transposition device in use, sometimes referred to as the third-position method, is that of identifying the viola as a violin, disregarding the difference in string names and reading each note in the alto clef a third lower than printed. This method offers an immediate reading technique but has the disadvantages of ignoring pitch and clef identification as well as confusing instruments and string names.

| Example II string (DEF) | Violinist's Interpretation II string (CDE) | Transposition a Third Lower II string (ABC) | Resulting Tones II string (DEF) |

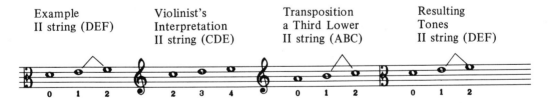

If the student attempts an association of sound to pitch name, he will be in error by the interval of a fifth. Further complications arise when the location of half-steps takes a capricious turn.

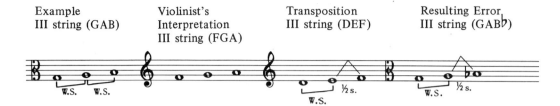

Example III string (GAB)	Violinist's Interpretation III string (FGA)	Transposition III string (DEF)	Resulting Error III string (GAB♭)

Devices such as this should be reserved for occasional use by experienced violinists who need immediate transposition but are willing to learn the alto clef at the earliest opportunity.

Position Chart for Viola

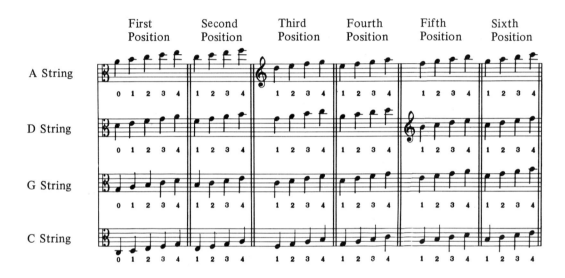

	First Position	Second Position	Third Position	Fourth Position	Fifth Position	Sixth Position

A String

D String

G String

C String

Changing Clefs

Composers and publishers have been remarkably inconsistent in following rules for clef changes. The violist must be prepared to follow the treble clef down to the "C" string and to count ledger lines in the alto clef in the higher positions. Contemporary composers have been particularly careless in this regard and may have deserved some of the wrong notes played by violists who had lost their bearings in unfamiliar territory. A general rule is to change clefs on or after C, preferably across the bar line.

Errors in reading may be expected at the change of clef since scale-line passages appear to contain a large intervallic leap. Far-sighted teachers will hold errors to a minimum by providing a drill to familiarize the student with this visual oddity.

Occasionally the violist is required to alternate clefs rapidly as in the following excerpt from Milhaud's "Sonata No. 1":

Example 28

Sonata no. 1   Milhaud

Harmonics

Violinists and violists alike require some instruction in reading harmonics. The diamond shaped note is used to indicate both natural harmonics (Example 29) and artificial harmonics (Example 30).

Example 29. Natural harmonics.

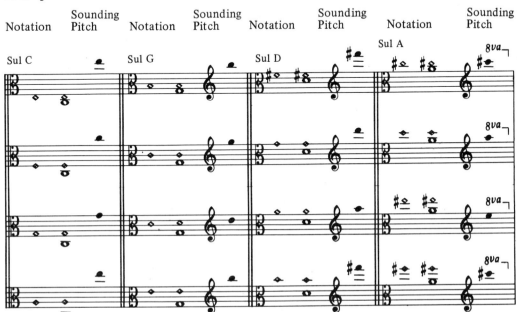

Example 30. Artificial harmonics.

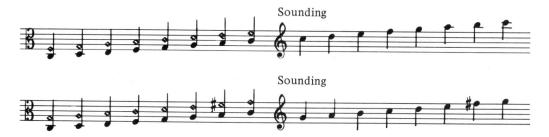

In both types, the diamond indicates the point at which the performer lightly touches the string, and is not the sounding point. Artificial harmonics involve the use of two fingers, the first fingered solidly and the fourth finger touching lightly at the interval of a fourth or a fifth (Example 30). Harmonics may be notated either by a small circle over the actual pitch point sounding the harmonic or by a diamond-shaped note at the pitch of a node producing the desired tone (Example 31).

Example 31

The entire series of natural harmonics is used in Stravinsky's *Le Sacre du Printemps* (Example 32).

Example 32

Le Sacre du Printemps   Stravinsky

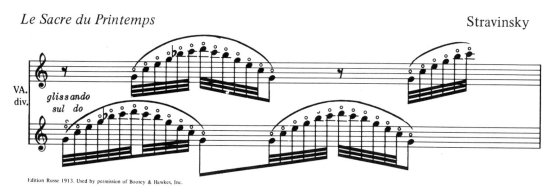

Edition Russe 1913. Used by permission of Boosey & Hawkes, Inc.

TRANSFERRING FROM VIOLIN TO VIOLA

From a violinist's point of view, the viola possesses specific negative qualities which are overcome only through dedicated effort, a classical example of the triumph of mind over matter. Played in the manner of a violin, the viola produces a shallow, flautato tone that is unpleasant and unsatisfying. Readily apparent to the performer is the fact that the viola's physical dimensions are incorrect for its tuning. Its ideal body length of twenty-one inches, correct for maximum resonance, is several inches too large for facile playing. The compromise of smaller instruments for comfort and facility in performance imposes tonal limitations and creates technical difficulties which must be overcome before satisfactory musical results are achieved (Illustration 1). Once all obstacles are dealt with, the viola becomes in the composer's words "an ideal medium for the expression of life's innermost feelings"—in the audience's response, "unmatched richness and beauty of tone"; and in the violist's reaction, "a perfect instrument for tapping the reservoir of man's culminating artistic achievement."

Illustration 1. Range of viola body sizes: 17-1/2″ model of a Gaspar da Salo; 16-3/8″ Landolphi; 14″ young beginner model. A graphic illustration of the necessity for fitting instrument to performer.

Summary of Negative Qualities and their Correction

Negative Qualities	Correction
Shallow tone, sluggish response	Use more left hand finger pressure and develop a wider, but not slower vibrato.
	Use more bow weight, particularly the natural pressure achieved through the use of the rotary motion of the forearm.
	Condition self to anticipate every entrance. Use a tape recorder with a slow playback speed to check out responses. The use of viola and metronome when taping will reveal on slow playback any lack of synchronization.
Unbalanced or unmatched quality of strings	Avoid stridency and nasal quality of the upper string through less pressure and a careful blend of sound with adjacent string.
	When feasible, adopt fingering to permit entire melodies to be played on one string.
	Use more extensions in fingering.
Tremendous distance to be covered when shifting	Requires extreme lightness of movement with concentration on scissor movement of elbow joint (see page 70).
	Use open strings and harmonics as an aid to quicker shifts.

Methods Designed for Changing from Violin to Viola

Bruni	Method	MZK, Ricordi
Iotti (Lamoureaux)	Practical Method	GS
Langey	Celebrated Tutor	CF
Laubach	Practical Viola School	Augener
Simon	From Violin to Viola	EdM
Spaulding	Viola for Violinists	Varitone
Tours	The Viola	Novello
Volmer	Bratschenschule	Schott
Wesseley	Practical Viola School	Williams
Whistler	From Violin to Viola	Rubank

LEFT-HAND TECHNIQUE

Writers in the field of string pedagogy have embraced, to some extent, the Gestalt psychology of teaching. In discussing left-hand technique, the interdependence of the fingers, wrist, elbow, arm, and body has called forth a total treatment of the subject with emphasis on a comfortable, balanced position and ease of performance.

The position of a performer, poised and ready to play, may be described. However, once movement begins, position becomes a dynamic, changing thing, making analysis extremely difficult. The position of the left hand will vary with fingering, string crossing, shifting, vibrato, trills, double stops, chords, arm and finger length, amount of pad on the finger tips, and musical requirements for expressive or articulated playing. For teaching purposes, the various units used in left-hand technique must be singled out for individual study.

Position in Performance

Hand

Position must be fluid to allow all fingers to reach their notes with ease.

Adjusts normally to aid the fingers in playing comfortably the interval of a fourth.

Center of balance is near the second and third fingers. Knuckle line is at a 30 or 40 degree angle to the viola neck, varying with the length of the little finger.

Is higher when on the C string, lower on the A.

Is higher for short arms and fingers.

Thumb

Assists in holding up the weight of the viola and in equalizing the downward pressure of the fingers.

Gives gentle support without gripping the neck of the viola.

Positioned toward the nail joint if the hand is large and when making extensions.

Positioned lower toward the palm if the hand is small and when making contractions.

In higher positions, placed under the neck of the viola near the thumb tip.

Usually placed opposite the first finger, the thumb may be moved between the first and second finger when the wrist is bent out for technical reasons.

Is often the source of tension in the hand.

Fingers

Drop vertically on the string with a movement from the base knuckles impelled by the larger arm muscles.

Should be aligned to the string so that the balance of the hand is near its center, favoring the little finger whose stretching potential is less than that of the first finger. (See Illustrations 2-4.)

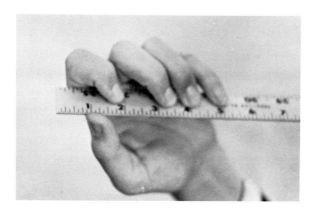

Illustration 2. Normal finger spacing.

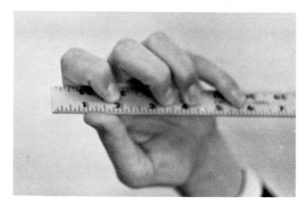

Illustration 3. Extension of fourth finger upward, approximately one-half inch.

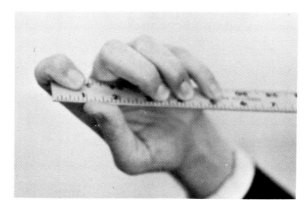

Illustration 4. Extension of first finger downward, approximately one inch.

64

Must be independent of each other at the base joint.

Should not touch each other except at the finger tip.

Wrist

Aligns the hand and arm in a straight line for normal playing in low positions.

May bend in slightly for chords, contracted finger patterns, half-positions, for trills and vibrato accents.

Must never collapse, a tendency encountered in beginning students.

Elbow

Position must be flexible varying with the string in play (to the left for higher strings, to the right for lower strings) and for articulation (to the right for percussiveness, to the left for a softer quality.

By swinging the elbow to the left and right under the viola, the player can see the advantages of each extremity and the need for continual adjustment. The choice lies between comfort of arm and efficiency of finger action.

Common Errors

The left arm, resting against the side of the body, is too far to the left to permit efficient finger placement.

The wrist rests against the viola neck in a collapsed position.

Neck of viola is allowed to drop into the slot between the thumb and forefinger.

Fingers approach the string obliquely rather than perpendicularly.

Thumb clutches the viola neck, inducing tension in the hand and arm.

Failure to swing the elbow to the right when moving to lower strings.

Failure to change finger angle in a stretching or contracting motion when changing finger patterns.

Failure to bring the hand higher when moving to a lower string.

Convulsive jerks of the left arm to match difficulties in bowing.

Keeping time with the left hand in an up and down motion.

Posture in Performance

Many experienced teachers would prefer to instruct a student from his very first lesson than to inherit another teacher's mistakes. Faced with a musical "cripple," the product of years of poor teaching and bad playing habits, the teacher is forced to assume the role of a physical therapist and to begin a program of retraining, a laborious process at best. Often this retraining can be shortened dramatically by concentrating on the improvement of posture, an approach that is equally effective with the beginning student.

Poor posture and bodily imbalance are the first factors that appear to inhibit freedom of movement and to reduce efficiency of response. The relationship of the head and neck to the rest of the body is of primary importance if a state of balanced equilibrium is to be achieved. Moving the neck and head out of line leads to compensatory postural deviations which are both stressful and unsightly.

Justification for this primary attention to posture is in the location in the neck of an unusually large number of proprioceptors, the internal receptors that receive sensations from the muscles, tendons, and joints and relay information concerning bodily balance to the central nervous system. It is the proprioceptors that aid the individual in determining position, the presence or absence of tension, and the impression of how a movement feels. These sensory impressions, along with gravity, balance, and leverage, are basic to all efficient motion.

At the first experience of holding the viola under his chin, the student is inclined either to retract his neck into his body in a crushing movement or to move his head out and down causing misalignment. A demonstration by the teacher that the head is capable of turning and tilting without disturbing the neck's alignment may help counteract this unfortunate tendency.

To assume a playing position, the individual turns his head slightly to the left and lowers his chin. He does not alter the position of his neck. He does not raise his shoulders.

A great deal of practice may be necessary in positioning and holding the viola in a comfortable, natural manner. If unusual tensions are permitted to arise at this point, they will spread like an epidemic when more complex movements are attempted.

Three Aspects of Left-Hand Technique:
Intonation, Shifting, Vibrato

Intonation

Out-of-tune playing is generally attributed to faulty technique or a poor ear. Improving the playing position and reducing muscular tension often clear up many intonation difficulties. A lack of pitch perception is a more serious matter. This deficiency may be due to the fact that the student has not discovered the relationship between consecutive tones. In many cases this discovery has been delayed by a lack of opportunity for musical experiences or by physical and social immaturity. Clearly implied in all references to intonation in the literature is the decided difference between hearing and listening. Hearing lacks the intense concentration found in critical listening. Lionel Tertis has written:

A good ear can become permanently perverted by negligent, superficial, non-penetrative listening on the part of the performer. This inattention in one's faculty of hearing is a vice of such rapid growth that in a very short time the player admits faulty intonation with equanimity, becoming quite unconscious that he is playing out of tune.[1]

It is the teacher's responsibility to determine whether the student is hearing pitches incorrectly or cannot remember them long enough to reproduce them accurately. Ear training may be the most essential part of a violist's education and must be stressed more in the case of some individuals than others.

The label assigned acceptable intonation by most professionals is "good." This is a misnomer in that intonation can never be an absolute. What may be considered "good intonation" in some situations would not be labeled "good" in others. Perhaps flexibility is the key word here. The inexperienced string player learns that when he plays with a piano he must adjust to the tempered scale. In an orchestra he has to adjust to the wind instruments, which are less flexible than the strings. Stringed instruments playing together use a harmonic tuning. When playing alone they raise and lower certain pitches to follow scale line tendencies. Adjustment of pitch in each of these situations will be small but absolutely essential.

The slight but necessary adjustments in intonation require highly critical listening, the development of a sensitivity to pitch relationships, the ability to think melodically and harmonically, and a rapid reaction rate in making adjustments in pitch. They also require a suspicious nature. It is a musical fact of life that what seemed in tune when practicing alone does not necessarily fit into the total harmonic sound when playing with a group.

Prerequisites to playing in tune:

> Good adjustment of instrument
> True strings testing perfect fifths
> Good hand position
> Knowledge of finger patterns
> Ability to transfer musical notation into finger patterns
> Understanding of finger angles and the stretching process necessary to raise and lower pitch
> Freedom of fingers at knuckle base to function independently of each other

Many factors influence intonation and contribute to insecurity and inaccuracy in performance. Physical control, mental awareness, and pitch sensitivity are the major areas to be considered in the development of fine pitch discrimination.

---

[1] Lionel Tertis, *Beauty of Tone in String Playing* (London: Oxford University Press, 1938), p. 11.

Physical Control

1. Excess speed. The performer has little time for analysis and correction and does not develop a feeling for tonality and the natural movement of scale tones.

   Encourage slow practice. Match badly out-of-tune pitches with the piano or make open string check.

2. Uncomfortable left-hand position preventing the natural dropping of the finger at a realistic angle to the string.

   Adjust the hand position, weighing size of hand, length of fingers, position of the elbow, string to be played, etc.

3. Poor orientation of the fingers to pitch locations on the fingerboard.

   Setting the hand position to conform with contour of viola neck and fingerboard. Molding hand to fit the perfect fourth interval. Developing a "feel" for finger patterns. Training cross-string fingering as well as ascending-descending fingering.

4. Slow correction of finger placement caused by tensions in the hand.

   Avoid clutching the neck of the viola. Eliminate the use of unneeded muscles. Tensions in the left hand may be sympathetically induced by tension in the bow arm. Fingers should slide easily to the correct pitch location.

5. Defects of the hand:

   A short little finger

   Dictates an upward adjustment of the entire hand for the convenience of the undersized member. This leads to a backward stretching of the longer fingers at a higher arc than normal and an adjustment of the arm to the right throwing the little finger over the string.

   Injured fingers

   Often requires an acrobatic adjustment of hand and arm in sympathy with finger movement or a refingering to avoid the incapacitated member.

   Webbed fingers

   Simple, non-exhausting stretching exercises to improve the elasticity of finger action.

   Weak fingers

   Strength building exercises (Example 33).

Example 33. Finger strengthener. Keep down unused fingers.

1. Poor concept of tonality in general and finger patterns in particular.

Theoretical training in scale formulas, interval spacing, intervals involving two strings and the canceled fifth (sixths fingered as seconds, sevenths as thirds, etc.).

Example 34. Finger pattern warm up.

2. Poor conception of distances when shifting.

Many repetitions of the same shift. Concentration on the extent of error. Loosening of the contact points to achieve a more effortless shift.

3. Lack of awareness of decreasing size of intervals in higher positions.

Scale practice in the upper positions.

4. Lack of awareness of the need for tempering and exaggerating intervals.

Theoretical training. Small ensemble playing. In general, play sharps high, flats low. M2, M3, M6, M7 wide openings; m2, m3, m6, m7 close spacing.

Example 35. Useful adjustment. First tune carefully.

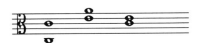

The octave, C, and the perfect fourth, E-A, place the fingers in position to play the major third, C-E, which will be tempered and a bit less consonant than the player may prefer.

5. Misconception of chordal patterns.

Sight singing. Imagine the missing scale notes.

6. Poor choice of fingering and unwise use of extensions and contractions.

Seek the most natural finger positions. Avoid shifting any higher than necessary. A rule of chromatic fingering: Half steps played with the same finger are wide apart; half steps played by consecutive fingers are close together.

7. Inability to think enharmonically.

Practice studies in multiple keys and enharmonic scales: F#-G♭, B-C♭, C#-D♭. Give special attention to contemporary music.

1. Inability to match pitches on the instrument.

   Requires vocalization. Student must internalize the pitch to be able to reproduce it. Set as a specific goal the development of a critical ear. Practice matching pitches and sight singing.

2. Failure to recognize resonance and clarity as important factors in intonation study.

   Adjust pitch to achieve maximum resonance. Learning to recognize the reinforcement effect of sympathetic vibrations. Associating clarity of sound with accuracy of pitch.

3. Inattention to need for immedaite adjustment of out of-tune pitch.

   Learning to accept each new pitch only in relation to preceding pitch. Improving pitch memory.

Double stops create particular physical as well as aural problems for the performer. Sixths, for example, are better played by sliding the fingers into place rather than lifting them. Fifths are more successfully played when the finger is centered more over the lower string, even to the extent of pulling the lower string toward the higher one. A flatter position of the fingers is an aid to truer fifths. The Bartók "Concerto" contains an extended passage of consecutive fifths, one of the most striking examples of the difficulty of performing this interval.

Example 36

Concerto   Bartók

Moderato, measures 160-162

© 1949 in U.S.A. by Boosey & Hawkes, Inc. Copyright for all countries. Used by permission of Boosey & Hawkes, Inc.

Shifting

Principles

The principles behind shifting are so simple that the teacher may wonder why students have so much difficulty with this technique. A student's lack of success may be attributed to two tendencies: not making mental or physical preparation before undertaking the shift; trying to shift the finger, not the hand or arm.

Shifting is an action of the arm with a follow-through of the hand and finger. A slight closing of the arm from the elbow joint results in an amazingly long and effortless trip for the finger in playing position. Concentration on the elbow movement takes the strain from shifting the finger from one position to another.

Preparing the shift is essential. The contact points, base of the first finger, thumb, and finger in play, must be loosened to reduce friction while the jaw and collar bone maintain a firm hold. The finger movement is anticipated by a slight motion in the hand and arm. A profitable practice is to shift without finger contact of the string in order to capture the sensation of unimpeded movement.

Procedure

Shift impelled by the bending of the elbow and controlled by the ear.

Left hand contact points lightened.

Anticipatory motion in the hand and arm before the finger leaves its position.

Gliding or sliding of the finger following the string line.

Using a flatter angle of the finger while shifting.

Maintaining the contour of the hand position and retaining the feeling of hand balance.

Matching speed of shift to speed of passage.

Holding out for full value the final note preceding shift.

Slowing the bow at the moment of shift in order to de-emphasize hand movement.

Sliding on the finger that is down, both ascending and descending, until the new position is reached, then dropping new finger in place. One exception to this principle is the taking over during the course of the slide of a lower finger which seeks the new position.

Giving particular attention to the quality of sound of the note preceding and the note climaxing the shift.

Common Errors	Correction
Permitting fingers to lead hand to new position	Focusing attention on closing motion of elbow and a leading or pre-motion of the arm.
Jerking or lurching toward the new position	Lightening the contact points. Anticipation of finger movement by a slight arm movement.
Unnecessary accents emphasizing change of position	Decrease of bow speed and pressure during the shift. Less finger pressure during change of position.
Pulling string out of line	Practice with the one purpose of following the string direction. Watch for tendency to push string to player's left.

Losing balance of hand while en route to new position

Special attention to the contour of hand position and the rhythm of the shift.

Speed of shift inappropriate to speed of passage

Make appropriate adjustment. The speed of the shift is one of the most important aspects of shifting and is frequently overlooked by students and teachers alike.

Failure to move out and over the ribs of the viola when shifting above third position (Illustration 5)

Care that the thumb assumes the role as guide in controlling the contour of the hand during position change.

Illustration 5. Setting hand for higher positions through pivotal action from the thumb tip.

Shifting conventions:

Shift on a half-step or in an established sequence of fingering, such as 123-123.

Shift on a strong beat so that the shift itself supplies the required rhythmical emphasis.

Shift as the bow reverses direction.

Shift in order to use similar fingerings of melodic sequences or on patterns repeated at the octave.

Shift when required by the musical content to retain the tone color of one string.

Shift preceding the quick notes of certain rhythmical figures, such as

Half-shift:

The use of extensions to avoid shifting as the thumb retains its position (Example 37).

Example 37

Study material for viola devoted to problems in shifting:

Applebaum	Second and Fourth Position String Builder	Belwin
	Third and Fifth Position String Builder	Belwin
Best	Early String Shifting	Varitone
Bornoff	Patterns in Position	Thompson
Gifford	12 Studies in the First, Second and Third Position	Augener
Johnson	Positions for All Strings	Varitone
Lukacs	Exercises in Change of Position	Kultura
MacKay	Position Changing for Viola	Oxford
Preston	Direct Approach to Higher Positions	Belwin
Sevcik	Changes of Position and Preparatory Scale Studies, op. 8	EV
	Changes of Position and Preparatory Scale Studies	Bosworth
Whistler	Introducing the Positions 2 vol.	Rubank

Covering great distances in a fast tempo is a problem on most musical instruments but is particularly awkward on the viola. Often a difficult passage will clear up miraculously when shifts are avoided and the hand assumes a compromise position as nearly in the center of the range of pitches as possible, as in this example from Arthur Benjamin's "Le Tombeau de Ravel."

Example 38

Le Tombeau de Ravel, measures 314–315   Benjamin

73

A trick of shifting at the moment of a harmonic, an octave above the open string, permits a quick adjustment of the hand to a lower position with no finger contacting the string at the moment of shift. The open string will sound an octave higher.

Example 39

Concerto   Walton
Vivo e molto preciso, measures 257-258

x = moment of shift

Extensions and contractions are used in the following passage to reach third position from seventh position with virtually no shifting:

Example 40

Variations for Four Drums and Viola   Colgrass

Vibrato

The vibrato is a facet of string playing that is as much related to temperament and taste as it is to technical development. In any large class a teacher will find students who develop a sensitive and beautiful vibrato with a minimum of instruction and those who must work very hard to develop any vibrato at all. Essential is the desire to learn to vibrate which begins with the hearing of a beautiful example and with the recognition of the vital, energizing quality that vibrato can add to otherwise cold playing.

Vibrato can be taught before the student feels the need for it, but the result may be mechanical and unsatisfying. Vibrato of this type is a controlled clock-wise action unrelated to expressiveness. The ultimate purpose of vibrato is to add variety and greater tonal beauty as well as to provide an avenue for emotional release. It is above all an individual matter related to personality and uniqueness of expression.

Procedure:

Approach vibrato calmly in a relaxed, not tense, state. Tension will produce irregularity and convulsiveness. Prepare movement with exercises away from the instrument stressing vibrato-like motions. In *Basic Principles of Violin Playing*[2] Paul Rolland recommends a conditioning exercise to be undertaken in three steps:

1. With both arms extended forward, hands palm down, thumb and index finger touching, shake both hands up and down to a narrow extent.
2. Repeat the motion in this position with the palms facing each other (horizontal shake).
3. Repeat the motion with the hands turned toward the face. Practice until the left-hand shake is as regular and controlled as the right-hand.

With the hand in third position—a starting point recommended by Flesch, Staelzing, Galamian, and others—continue the controlled oscillation with only the base of the hand in contact with the body of the instrument. Check the movement for regularity of cycle and for freedom from tension.

Continue oscillation with thumb in position and with second finger lightly touching the D string, sliding back and forth several inches propelled by wrist shake. *Avoid contact of forefinger base with the neck of the viola.* This position would lock the hand in position and restrict freedom of movement.

Gradually narrow the oscillation until the finger rests in one spot, rocking back and forth on the tip. With the finger lightly pressing the string in playing position, continue the wrist shake. Avoid clutching the instrument. Check for evenness and control, equal distance on backward and forward swing, and direction of the oscillation (parallel to the string). Unevenness may be caused by poor coordination or by tension in the arm. Gradually increase speed in rhythm, as follows:

Continue silent exercises with the first, third, and fourth fingers. Remove contact of base of hand with the body of the viola.

Practice vibrato in first position (Illustration 6).

In the case of unusual stiffness in the fingers:

Press the scroll against the wall to provide support in holding the viola and freeing the left hand for vibrato action.

Practice trills with very light pressure to free up finger action.

Practice shifting of the hand to neighboring positions leaving the thumb in place.

Practice vibrato while holding the viola in other positions, such as under the arm, guitar-fashion.

---

[2]Paul Rolland, *Basic Principles of Violin Playing,* (Washington: The MENC String Instruction Committee, 1959).

Illustration 6. Supporting the hand beginning vibrato in first position.

Common Errors	Correction
Locking hand to neck of viola	Releasing support of the hand, at the base of the forefinger. This point must not touch the viola during vibrato.
Irregular or convulsive pulsation	Probably due to tensions in the arm. Begin oscillation again with the instrument. Stress ease and evenness of movement. Do not attempt to speed up vibrato until ease of movement is assured.
Attempting to vibrate at right angle to the string	Slide the finger up and down the string. Compel the first joint of the finger to bend with the hand movement in the direction of the string (Illustrations 7 and 8).
Excessive arm vibrato	Useful in double stops, particularly octaves, arm vibrato can be controlled by third-position practice, blocking arm movement by touching the viola body with the base of the hand.

Variety of Tone Color

It is possible to develop a vibrato that will be largely centered in the fingers, the hand, or the arm. A combination of three movements offers the player greater contrast in musical shading and more individuality in sound. Experimentation in

Illustration 7. Starting position in the vibrato cycle.

Illustration 8. Flattened finger position in the vibrato cycle.

slight changes of speed, varying widths of movement, and tiny delays in starting movement will add variety and contrast in expression.

Books and Studies Emphasizing Vibrato

Eberhardt, Siegfried	*Violin Vibrato*	CF
Flesch, Carl	*Art of Violin Playing,* Vol. 1	CF
Galamian, Ivan	*Principles of Violin Playing and Teaching*	Prentice-Hall
Leland, Valborg	*Dounis Principles of Violin Playing*	CF
Leviste, Roger	*Rational Technic of Vibrato*	Bosworth
Rolland, Paul	*Basic Principles of Violin Playing,* String Instruction Program no. 10	MENC
Staelzing	*Basic Vibrato Studies*	Belwin

RIGHT-HAND TECHNIQUE

Motion in Bowing

Basic motions of the bow arm have been described in the works of Flesch, Berkley, and Galamian. These motions, seldom performed singly, depend on the interrelationship of all muscles and joints of the arm working together in complete accord. The interdependence of these units must not be overlooked although various parts of the bowing apparatus may be consciously isolated in practice in order to develop flexibility and to cultivate the correct sensation for particular movements. Great care must be exercised in the isolation and development of certain motions that have a normally passive function; the hand and finger movement, for example. An important guiding principle is that larger muscles be used for major bowing functions, with smaller muscles being reserved for subtle articulations.

Functions of the Bowing Units

Upper Arm:

> Vertical motion from the shoulder
>> Used in string crossing.
>
> Horizontal motion from the shoulder joint
>> Used in the lower half of the bow.
>
> Oblique and curved motions
>> Combination of vertical and horizontal motions used in crossing strings in legato bowings.
>
> Supplementary
>> Supporting the lower arm and transmitting power from the body muscles.

Forearm:

Horizontal or open-closed motion from the elbow
In drawing the bow in the upper half.
In subtle reversing action to the direction of the bow change.
Rotary motion from the elbow
In approaching and leaving the string.
In transferring power of larger muscles to the string.
In repeated string crossings combined with vertical movement of the hand.

Hand:

Vertical motion from the wrist joint
In adjusting the height of the wrist.
In repeated string crossings often combined with the rotary motion of the forearm.
In bowings requiring the movement of small muscles, the flying spiccato, and the flying staccato, for example.
Horizontal motion
In change of bow direction.
Circular motion
A combination of vertical and horizontal movement, as in sautillé bowing.

Fingers:

Vertical motion
In rapid string crossings
In flying staccato and spiccato and ricochet bowings.
Horizontal motion
In change of bow.
Combinations
Circular motions, horizontal and vertical, that aid the control of bow pressure, angle, string crossings, etc.
Extended-curved motions
In martelé bowing, fingers on the down-bow change from curved to extended position. The reverse is true on the up-bow.

Types of Bowing

On-The-String Legato

Legato. Sustained, connected stroke with virtually inaudible bow change. Applies to slurred notes or long notes in a slow tempo.

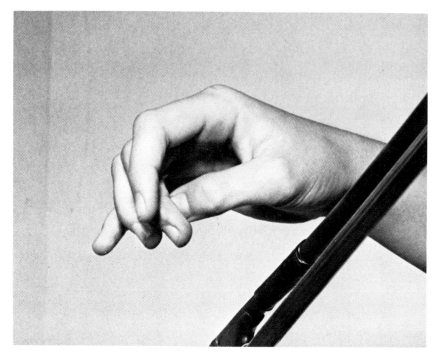

Illustration 9. Step by step placement of the fingers on the bow (see Illustrations 10-12).

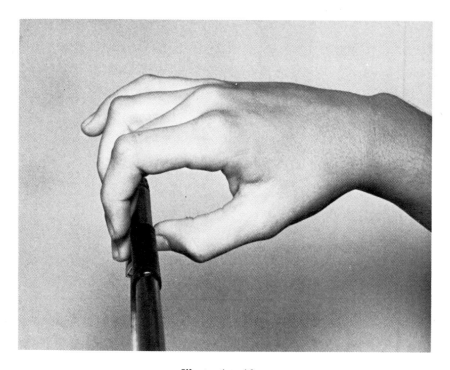

Illustration 10.

80

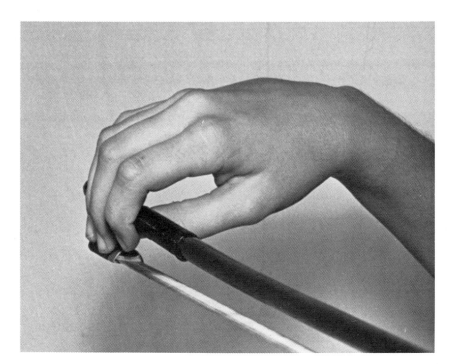

Illustration 11.

Illustration 12.

81

Portato, Louré, Ondulé, Inflecto. ♩ ♩ ♫♫ One or more notes on each stroke, smoothly connected but individually articulated by a fluctuation in bow pressure.

Detaché. ♫ ♫♫ Smooth separate bows concealing the change of bow with no change of pressure.

Detaché porté. ♩ ♩ An impression of separation due to increased pressure and speed at the beginning of each note. An inflection more than an accent.

Detaché lancé. ♩ A short stroke with great initial speed dissipating toward the end of the stroke. Similar in character to martelé but with less accent.

Fouetté (Whipped). ♪ ♪ Striking the string from the air to add a strong initial attack. Often used up-bow when a decisive attack is desired.

Principles:

A preparatory motion, as in a silent up-bow or a breathing in, is necessary to overcome inertia and to initiate the legato stroke.

The bow should be drawn parallel to the bridge despite the natural tendency to move in a clockwise curve.

Common Fault   Correction

Bow pressure, speed of bow, and point of contact on the string are variable factors that must be controlled if a sustained legato is to be developed.

Change of bow is initiated in the upper arm, the hand and fingers being the last to participate in the change of direction.

A reduction in bow speed at the change of direction helps conceal the change.

Most bowing motions, including change of direction, are circular in character and should be taught as such (see page 84).

Pedagogy:

Instruction in bowing should begin with the simplest possible movements and should be directed toward the acquiring of a feeling for specific, basic motions that are in constant use.

From the beginning seek a resonant, concentrated tone. Never permit the bow to slide or skim along the string even in soft passages. Build a concept of pulling tone from the viola. Use similar speed and pressure going into consecutive patterns.

Impart the principle of domination by larger muscles and passive follow through by smaller units of the bow arm.

Give special attention to the early introduction of basic circular motions. A silent pivoting over all four strings without a horizontal movement shows this circular path clearly and demonstrates the domination of motion by the upper arm and the passive follow through of the smaller units of the bow arm.

Even elementary material contains problems in string crossing which call for early development of circular motions, as in the following example:

Example 41

LÄNDLER (Grade 2)   Mozart-Carruthers

Common Faults	Correction
Accenting the first note	Place bow on the string with the same pressure required by the stroke itself.
Accented bow changes	Reduce speed and lift pressure at the change of bow. Avoid overly active finger motion.
Non-legato connection of bow	Follow a circular path, drawing frog of bow toward player at change of direction (Diagram 1).

Diagram 1. Player's view looking toward fingerboard.

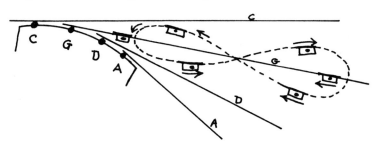

Defective string crossing , Preparing bow by moving near the new string to be played. Advance placement of the new finger to be used.

Movements of the Right Hand

Example	Student's Misconception	Correction

Player's view looking toward fingerboard

Example	Student's Misconception	Correction

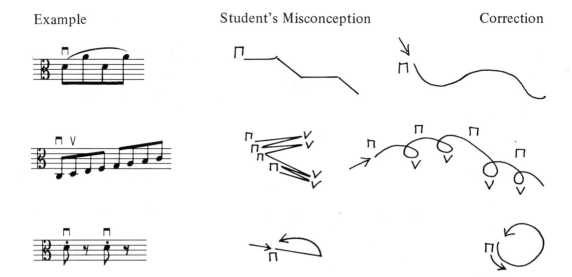

The above patterns have their reversals in similar examples beginning up-bow.

On-The-String Marcato

Martelé (hammered). Preliminary pressure, pinching the string, is released at the moment of the stroke. The attack is crisp; the release, abrupt. A rest between strokes.

Staccato. A term used, in a general sense, for all short notes and, specifically, for a series of martelé strokes in the same direction.

Accented detaché. Strong accents emphasize the change of bow. An excellent stroke for developing clarity of sound.

Serré (crowded). A form of accented detaché. Strongly accented with little bow.

Picqué (spurred). The shortest staccato stroke consisting almost entirely of a martelé attack. Performed by straightening and recurving the fingers. Also may be classified as an off-the-string bowing.

Principles:

Staccato bowing aids articulation and tone projection and helps develop consciousness of bow division and a strong rhythmic sense.

Pressure is applied by means of forearm rotation before the motion begins.

Release of pressure and initial burst of speed are simultaneous.

Space between notes depends on a gradual dissipation of motion similar to coasting rather than a braking action of opposing muscles.

Marcato action is initiated in the entire arm with the fingers straightening on the downward motion and recurving on the upward motion.

Staccato is performed as a series of martelé strokes in the same direction of the bow.

Pedagogy:

A preliminary application and release of pressure without moving the bow demonstrates the correct feeling for marcato bowing. Observe depression of the string. Speed in applying the pressure-release movement can be acquired prior to a first attempt of this important bowing.

In order to produce a marcato of good quality, the initial pressure must be released at the beginning of the bow stroke.

Use a small section in the middle of the bow before lengthening the stroke.

When performing down-bow staccato, drop the wrist and elbow below the frog and tilt the stick toward the bridge. The reverse is true for up-bow staccato. Limit staccato practice to short intervals of time to avoid fatigue.

Typical Faults	Correction
Scratchy tone quality due to failure to release pressure	Emphasize release in initial movement and the effect of coasting to a gradual stop. Lift bow on approaching the frog on the up-bow.
Insufficient accent	Caused by a lack of pressure or the premature release of pressure. Make the appropriate adjustment. Upward pressure of the thumb or a general pinching of the bow by all fingers will improve the accent.
Tension in the bow arm	Eliminate the use of opposing muscles. Avoid active hand participation. Seek a power source in the larger muscles.
Poor coordination between staccato bowing and left hand action	Practice staccato bowing on open string until correct speed is achieved, then add fingering.

The Baroque style of playing demands staccato eighth notes. A demonstration of the difference in character of the opening of the Telemann "Concerto" in G major (Example 42) played legato and then staccato should be quite a revelation to the student. Staccato eighths give the music lightness, buoyancy and rhythmical drive. Legato eighths completely destroy the Baroque style.

Example 42

Concerto in G   Telemann

Allegro, measures 7-8

In minimizing difficult string crossings during staccato passages a useful technique is to come to rest on the new string to be played. As the bow coasts to a stop it is moved silently to its new position with complete muscular relaxation. Example 43 is an excellent study for martelé practice and for developing a straight bow and a flexible bow hand.

Example 43

Sonata no. 5   Vivaldi

Allegro, measures 3-6

Off-The-String

Spiccato. ♩♩♩ The bow, which is held with a very light grip of the fingers, is thrown on the string. In a fast tempo, the bow rebounds of its own accord. In a slower tempo, the rebound is aided by a lifting motion with the arm in a higher than normal position.

Sautillé. ♩♩♩ An automatic bouncing created by a quick tempo and the natural resiliency of the stick. Motion is centered in the fingers and hand moving in an oblique direction.

Staccato volante (flying staccato). A series of up-bow spiccatos using a solid staccato motion with light pressure permitting the bow to leave the string after each note. The bow may be dropped on the string or the movement begun on the string, staccato, with a lifting of the arm and the use of a vertical hand motion.

Ricochet, Jeté. A series of down-bow spiccatos initiated by one thrown stroke, the resilience of the bow providing the impulse for successive notes. To an extent uncontrolled, the ricochet may be partly governed by its location on the stick and by the height of the bounce.

Principles:

The bow, due to its resilience, will bounce in a predictable way if all conditions are right. An absolute evenness of bow stroke and an unbroken continuity are prerequisites to good spiccato.

Slow spiccato requires a throwing down of the bow.

Fast spiccato (sautillé) requires a bounce growing from the detaché stroke and leading to the next bounce.

Placing the stick directly above the bow hair makes better use of the bow's resiliency.

Keeping the bounce close to the string gives more control.

The amount of arm movement needed is in inverse proportion to the speed of the spiccato.

Pedagogy:

Slow spiccato

Of general practice is the use of the vertical drop without a horizontal movement near the balance point as a first step. This motion encourages the player to relinquish control over the bow and to develop a "feel" for the bow's natural bounce. The bow must not be gripped. The student's attention should be directed toward the fact that the bounce is dependent more on the bow's inherent springiness than on the lowering and raising of the arm. The resistance of the string will kick back the bow to the starting position if enough impulse is applied to the drop. Next, add the horizontal motion by striking the string obliquely. Percussiveness can be controlled by adjusting the height of the drop and the length of the horizontal stroke. The arm must lead and the hand must follow.

Fast spiccato

Approach sautillé from a detaché stroke in the middle of the bow. Begin slow, even strokes, then increase speed. As tempo increases, shift weight of the hand to the little finger and begin an oblique motion, more down and up than back and forth. Add an accent to the first note of each group of four or eight.

A second method used by many teachers is to begin a tremolo movement in the upper part of the bow, then let the bow drift until it reaches the balance point. To reduce fatigue, practice short mixed patterns similar to the following:

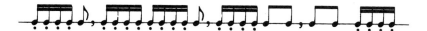

Experience is needed playing at various speeds and dynamic levels and with quick changes of speed. Frequently a better quality of sautillé results when some bow hair remains on the string.

Typical Faults	Corrections
The student cannot relinquish his control over the bow	Lighten the bow hold and practice the rotary motion of the forearm and the vertical drop.
Uneven movement of the bow	Slow detaché practice measuring the distance traveled up bow and down bow.
The bow will not leave the string	Check for evenness of bow stroke, flexibility of grip, and direction of stroke. Emphasize bow's ability to bounce. Add a strong accent in an oblique direction to each group of notes. Check to see that weight of the hand is shifted toward the little finger.
The section of the bow in use is incorrect for the speed of the spiccato	As the tempo increases, the bounce is more effective nearer the point.

Bowing Conventions

Down-bow

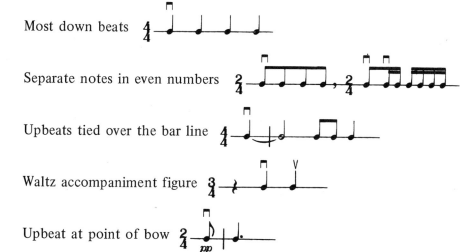

Slurred and hooked bowings in even numbers

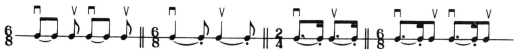

89

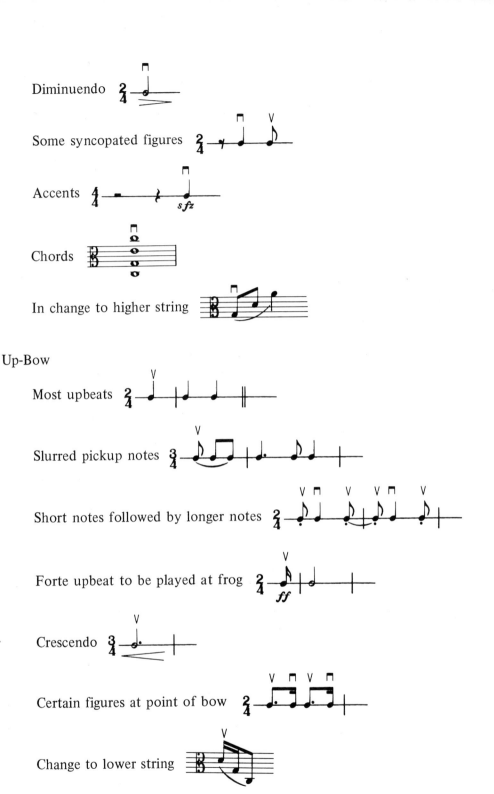

Diminuendo

Some syncopated figures

Accents

Chords

In change to higher string

Up-Bow

Most upbeats

Slurred pickup notes

Short notes followed by longer notes

Forte upbeat to be played at frog

Crescendo

Certain figures at point of bow

Change to lower string

Plan the bowing in relation to what is to follow. This may necessitate changing a bowing convention. If needed, take more than one bow on long notes. Change bow whenever possible on the change of position or change of string. Accent only the beginning of a syncopation. In a quick tempo rest on the tied note

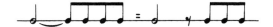

Typical Bowing Variations for Use with Scales and Studies

The varied scale passages found in solo, orchestral, and chamber music literature require flexibility in fingering and bowing. Scales should be practiced beginning on tones other than the tonic. The "D" major scale below indicates alternate fingerings which are universally accepted and are to be played with standard bowing patterns.

22-Note Scale

24-Note Scale

Books Analyzing Bowing Problems

Babitz, Sol	*Differences Between 18th Century and Modern Bowing*	ASTA
Berger, Melvin	*Basic Viola Technique*	MCA
Berkley, Harold	*Modern Technique of Violin Bowing*	GS
Dolejsi, Robert	*Modern Viola Technique*	ASTA
Galamian, Ivan	*Principles of Violin Playing and Teaching*	Prentice-Hall
Hodgson, Percival	*Motion Study and Violin Bowing*	ASTA
Rolland, Paul	*Basic Principles of Violin Playing,* String Instruction Program no. 10	MENC
Rosenberg, Fred	*Violin: The Technique of Relaxation and Power*	ASTA
Shirley, Paul	*Right Hand Culture*	CF

THREE APPROACHES TO STRING STUDY

The beginning string teacher, possessing little experience and few convictions, may consider profitably several types of teaching methods as a starting point in building a philosophy of string teaching. Types of methods which readily come to mind are those featuring a rhythmical approach, a direction of motion approach and a Gestalt approach as major areas of emphasis. Selecting a combination of the best elements emphasized in these approaches would be superior to the acceptance of any one method.

The Rhythmical Approach

The concept of rhythm as sound moving toward a destination offers the teacher a pedagogical tool that has focus and direction. The simple process of playing through from the first to the last notes in a passage insures phrase-wise direction and forces details into place. Less important factors may be subordinated in the beginning to a fundamental and pervasive rhythm. A rhythmical emphasis improves timing and synchronization and assures continuity and the elimination of stumbling.

The rhythmical approach emphasizes exercises and drills within the framework of the program of study. Variations of familiar melodies in rhythm, preparatory gymnastic drills with the bow, early introduction of staccato bowing, and the use of rote materials all give the student a feeling of security in bow balance and control and freedom in rapid bow movements.

The teacher may favor confining his use of rhythms to the simple basic ones used in the Suzuki approach or moving through the tortuous variations of Ševčik's opus 2. While there is a pleasure in repeating a satisfying experience, repeated activities become routine and eventually boring. Study and practice must seem interesting enough to the student to justify the expenditure of his time and effort.

Direction of Motion Approach

The leading exponent of the direction of motion approach is the English pedagog, Percival Hodgson, who classified bowing movements as being across the strings, around the strings, and away from the strings.[3] Having taken thousands of cyclographs Hodgson is convinced that the bow does not move in straight lines and that bowing curves fall into definite types which should be taught. From the first step of silently rocking the bow across four strings to demonstrate the circular path of the hand and the upper arm as the controlling level, Hodgson moves into slurred bowings as a beginning technique. This approach trains the whole arm to function as a unit and delimits the bow level for a single string as being within the total curved pattern. The upper arm is accorded complete freedom, and correctly proportioned pivoting movements around the strings are assured.

Although Hodgson's book presents a mechanistic approach to string playing, his careful analysis of the structure and function of bone and muscle is an aid to the teacher working to reduce tension in the performance of young violists. Two general principles of importance may be inferred from Hodgson's writing:

1. The larger muscles and limbs should dominate the playing apparatus.
2. Muscles, which are paired, must never be used simultaneously to oppose each other.

---

[3]Percival Hodgson, *Motion Study and Violin Bowing* (Urbana: American String Teachers Association, 1958).

The basic movements considered by Hodgson are allowed to follow the natural demands of gravity and centrifugal force. Bowing is described as consisting of free wheeling with rest points, much as the movement of a pendulum.

Gestalt Approach

F. A. Steinhausen[4] was the first physician to examine string playing from the viewpoint of biomechanics. He pointed out, as basic mistakes in method books of his day, the failure to emphasize muscular relaxation and the tendency to encourage motions that were too small. The major objective, as Steinhausen saw it, was the reduction of tension in the joints of the smaller units by assigning control to the main joints, the shoulder and the elbow. No part-motions were permitted to interfere with the pattern of whole motion.

Studies by Polnauer[5] conclude that there is a need for a reevaluation of string teaching and a move away from the the traditional "right" and "left" hand technique toward a concept of "total body" technique. The influence of other body-parts on the left and right hand during performance is treated in detail by Polnauer and Marks in their scientific treatise, *Senso-Motor Study and Its Application to Violin Playing,*[6] a landmark in the reconciliation of string playing to Gestalt theory.

As applied to viola teaching, the Gestalt approach not only refers to the playing mechanism as a whole but to the method of introducing whole facets of technique. Slurring, full bows, staccato and spiccato, and multiple finger patterns are made a part of the technique as soon as possible. A strong point in favor of this approach is the variety it offers to pique the beginner's interest. The consolidation and refinement of technique acquired so rapidly is another problem, however.

---

[4]F. A. Steinhausen, *Die Physiologie der Bogenfuehrung* (Leipzig: Breitkopf & Haertel, 2. Aufl. 1907).

[5]F. F. Polnauer, "Biomechanics, a new approach to music education" *Journal of the Franklin Institute,* Vol. 254, No. 4, 1952.

[6]F. F. Polnauer and Morton Marks, *Senso-Motor Study and its Application to Violin Playing* (Urbana: American String Teachers Association, 1964).

Chapter III

PEDAGOGIC ASPECTS OF TEACHING VIOLA

THE LEARNING PROCESS

All definitions of learning emphasize the interaction of the individual with his environment. Although learning cannot be observed, a change in performance is an indication that learning has taken place. Some psychologists view learning as a mental process of forming, strengthening, or weakening associative connections between stimuli and responses, while others identify the development of insights as the main element in learning.

Although there is disagreement as to the precise changes that occur in the individual when learning takes place, there is a rather general agreement about the conditions and practices that are effective in promoting learning. These factors are summed up effectively in Hilgard's principles of learning, which have been extended and freely adapted here to cover instrumental music study.[1]

Principles of Learning Applicable to Music Study

People are not only educable but have potentials far greater than has been realized. In few other areas of learning does the realization of an individual's potential rest so heavily on a single teacher as in the area of music. The student generally returns to the same teacher year after year, making him the key person in determining the extent to which potential is realized. Recognizing the fact that an individual's contact with music may be terminated through frustration and disappointment or may open rewarding new avenues for a lifetime of pleasure should cause the teacher to reflect on his responsibility in the learning process.

Since the student's attention is a response, the skilled instructor works to aid him in developing concentration. This ability may develop as a result of the teacher's contagious positive attitudes and businesslike approach to the problems at hand with no time wasted through a discussion of non-musical matters. Concentration is also controlled by tailoring the lessons to each individual's own rate of development.

---

[1] Ernest T. Hilgard, *Theories of Learning,* 2nd Edition (New York: Appleton-Century Crofts, Inc., 1956).

The learning process may be accelerated through the use of musical materials and activities that are meaningful to the student. Transfer of learning takes place better if the learner is led to discover the relationship himself.

The importance of motivation must not be overlooked. The motivated student learns more readily. The experience of success in musical study will strengthen motivation and a backlog of success will make it easier to handle an occasional experience of failure. However, it must be kept in mind that excessive motivation may induce emotional stress.

Learning is a process of clarifying and achieving goals. Students need both experience and guidance in setting realistic goals for themselves. Learning tasks may have to be separated into component parts for analysis, which is not likely to occur without the assistance of a skilled teacher. The instructor, by scaling the task to the learner's physical and intellectual ability, helps him learn more rapidly and more permanently.

The learning process takes place more readily when it aids the adjustment and the social growth of the individual. Learning is further aided when the student understands the nature of a good performance, the nature of his own mistakes, and the progress that he is making.

To achieve ease and security in musical performance, it is necessary that overlearning take place as a result of repetitive practice. This overlearning is highly recommended for public performance and memorization.

The Role of Practice in the Learning Process

Seldom can learning take place in viola study as the result of one response to a stimulus. Thorndike's Law of Exercise, often called the law of "use and disuse," emphasizes the necessity for practice in learning and the deterioration of performance when practice is neglected.

Practice in itself, however, does not lead to improvement but may lead to deterioration of the activity practiced. The crucial ingredient is not the motivation to practice but the motivation to improve performance. Understanding (insight) and the will to learn must be present to insure the making of an improved response. One of the justifications for repetitive practice is the chance that a favorable variation in performance will result.

The teacher should be concerned with the student's ability to observe and evaluate the consequences of his acts. Insight reduces the need for blind groping for a correct response and hastens effect-producing behavior. This can be the only "short-cut" in improving musical performance.

Generalizations regarding motivated practice in reading literature, which apply equally well to instrumental practice, have been summed up by Smith and Dechant as follows:[2]

---

[2]Henry P. Smith and Emerald V. Dechant, *Psychology in Teaching Reading* (Englewood Cliffs: Prentice-Hall, Inc., 1961) pp. 62-63.

Practice does not itself cause learning; it merely provides time for whatever does cause learning.

In general, distributed practice is more efficient than massed practice.

Members of a group tend to become more different rather than more alike as a result of practice.

Generally, the greater a child's rate of learning, the less practice is necessary for learning.

The implications for the viola teacher are clear. Practice without motivation will not lead to improvement in performance. Motor skills generally improve faster with spaced rather than massed practice. However, the slow learner may require massed practice in order to have time to perceive relationships. Individual differences dictate a change in amount and kind of practice for each student.

Motivation as an Aid to the Learning Process

Attitudes toward learning control achievement to a large degree. An individual's desire to learn and his willingness to commit himself to sustained effort may make the difference between success and failure in viola study. Viola teachers in the United States rate motivation above musical aptitude among the minimum standards which they apply before accepting prospective students. So important is motivation that some psychologists include it as an essential part of intelligence.

Bugelski states: "Motives are themselves responses to stimuli; they do not arise spontaneously or independently in the absence of stimuli; they are like habits in this respect, and like habits, must be thought of as organized patterns laid down in the nervous system through a process of training."[3] Baller and Charles, in reviewing the beliefs of a number of psychologists, conclude that "in the individual there is a basic tendency toward making actual that which is potential in him."[4] These views of motivation place on the teacher the responsibility of aiding the individual in acquiring a creative attitude, in accumulating good work habits, and in achieving self-realization.

To a degree, motivation is controlled by a person's image of himself, his estimate of his potential, and his experience with success. Bernard states: "How one perceives a situation is influenced by how he perceives himself."[5] Anderson feels that "the pattern of life of every individual is a living out of his self-image; it is his road map for living."[6]

---

[3]B. R. Bugelski, *An Introduction to the Principles of Psychology* (New York: Rinehart & Company, Inc., 1960) p. 142.

[4]Warren R. Baller and Don C. Charles, *The Psychology of Human Growth and Development* (New York: Holt, Rinehard and Winston, 1961), p. 142.

[5]Harold W. Bernard, *Psychology of Learning and Teaching*, 2nd Edition (Englewood Cliffs: Prentice-Hall, Inc., 1965) p. 25.

[6]Camille M. Anderson, "The Self-Image," *Mental Hygiene*, Vol. 36 (1952), pp. 227-244.

A great many beliefs about self are accumulated over a period of years, particularly in childhood. Evaluations of self are often founded on fears of inadequacy. When imaginary, these feelings lead to repeated failure in performance and are self-inflicted, so to speak. The experienced teacher will find that he can exercise control in many ways over the student's self-image, the extent of his motivation, and the number of his experiences of success.

Aids to Motivation in Music Study

If the teacher exhibits skill in teaching and an infectious spirit of enthusiasm, no further aid to motivation is required. Skilled teachers clarify goals and the meaning of achievement. They present a sequence of material that is logical, uniform, and gradual enough to insure progress, with the new related to what is known. The skilled teacher aids the student in forming a clear mental picture of a correct response and shapes poor responses to facilitate their correction. Corrections are made in a helpful way and poor habits are eliminated. Learning is promoted through public performance and the student is appraised of progress. Last and most important, the student's self-image is improved.

LEARNING DIFFICULTIES

The Slow Learner

More strongly motivated by praise than by criticism, the slow learner requires patience, kindness, and understanding on the part of the teacher. Short-term goals, immediate rewards, and encouragement are effective devices in working with the less gifted. Drills on fundamentals and repetitions in different contexts also aid development. Specific instructions are necessary. The slow learner wants to be told what to do. Used to failure and easily discouraged, he needs a better chance for success than do his more gifted peers. Having experienced limited success, he will try for a higher goal only if he is given reason to think that he can succeed. His learning experiences must be geared to success and to the building of confidence.

Learning sequences must be broken down into the smallest units for this type of student. Since he needs more experience than others in the physical manipulations involved in instrumental performance, more than the usual amount of rote teaching is indicated. Only when the student is at ease with his instrument should music reading be introduced.

The slow learner feels the need for the security of remaining at one level longer than the average student. He is more content to play simple materials than to undergo the frustration of struggling with difficult assignments. Success experiences are further increased by the wise use of more review than for the average or the gifted student. Approaches to the slow learner may be summarized as follows:

Learn away from the instrument.

Use a performance-readiness plan to help eliminate mistakes before they arise.

Employ rote teaching.

Make goals relatively immediate.

Offer detailed but simplified explanations.

Require many repetitions for full comprehension.

Use more review.

Use carefully graded materials.

Motor-Control and Tension in Performance

Individuals differ in degrees of coordination from highly coordinated to very clumsy. The student with severe problems of motor control will have difficulty in adjusting to music study. The studies of Delacato[7] suggest that many cases of poor coordination are the result of poor neurological organization. Some authorities feel that difficulties of motor control stem from faulty patterns of lateral dominance (preferred sidedness) such as crossed dominance, a condition in which the dominant hand and eye are on the opposite sides of the body, and mixed dominance in which there is uncertainty as to the preferred hand.[8] Motor control generally improves with age and can be improved with practice. Although students who experience severe cases of motor incoordination will have to be referred to more qualified therapists, the viola teacher should feel an obligation to instruct the less-gifted. In many cases, the private music lesson will provide the most intensive personalized and diagnostic training that a student will receive during the course of his entire education.

Efficiency in movement implies the use of the least possible effort to achieve desired results and is a primary objective in musical performance. Skeletal muscles are usually identified in pairs counterbalancing the action of the joint which they control. It is extremely important that contraction or shortening should occur in only one muscle of the pair at a time. Due to overstimulation during public performance, there is a tendency to contract muscles indiscriminately and to fail to inhibit antagonistic muscles. Coordinated patterns of contraction and inhibition must be well conditioned against interference under stress. Overexertion introduces competing behavior. The analysis of complex movements and the development of kinesthetic imagery, the ability to project oneself into a pattern, are areas in which most viola students need guidance. An understanding of basic principles of movement and types of defective motion will lead to more effective teaching.

---

[7]Carl H. Delacato, *The Diagnosis and Treatment of Speech and Reading Problems* (Springfield, Illinois: Charles C. Thomas Publisher, 1963).

[8]Albert J. Harris, *Harris Tests of Lateral Dominance, Manual of Directions,* 3rd ed. (New York: The Psychological Corporation, 1958).

Principles of Movement

Mechanical laws of gravity, balance, motion, leverage, and force are basic to efficient motion. Teachers frequently use the term "relaxation" to explain coordination. While some tension is necessary in movement, static tension is damaging. Although movement is a natural function not completely controlled by thought, the individual can be trained to become aware of the kinesthetic aspect of experience. Individuals have a natural propensity for certain motions; other motions have to be developed.

Improving performance is a process of eliminating unnecessary and ineffective effort. Motion initiated by instinct is rarely as efficient as motion controlled by reason. Defective movements that are not consciously blocked will slip back into old patterns. When retraining, the old response to stimuli must be inhibited before the new behavior patterns can be developed.

Types of Defective Motion

Wrong sources of power (misdirection)
Too many muscles in use (competing behavior)
Use of opposing muscles functioning as brakes and causing static tension
Exceeding optimum tension required for task
Application of force in the wrong direction
Muscular indecision due to sketchy knowledge of basic technic
Lack of reservoir of strength due to poor conditioning
Sympathetic tension induced by overexertion
Lack of uniformity in muscle use

Common Defective Motions Applied to Viola Performance

Only close observation of performance over a long period will clarify the points above. Excessive movement of the body or a rigid position of the viola under the chin are sure clues to poor muscular use. Fingers pressing into the string past the point required to sound a clear tone may be felt rather than seen. Excessive shifting because of poor fingering or shifting higher than is necessary to satisfy musical requirements are clues to the poor use of motion in performance. Straight and stiff joints are readily apparent, but the use of antagonistic muscles may be deduced by observation. Facial contortions may be seen by all, but unnecessary lifting of fingers requires closer scrutiny. Bow pressure produced by vertical rather than rotary movement is movement of the wrong kind. Other examples of inefficient movement include active finger motion in changing direction of the bow, the use of straight line rather than circular bowing patterns (see page 84), and changing strings from center of string level rather than close zoning (Diagram 1, page 83).

TEACHING TECHNIQUE

Good Teaching Technique

Progress in viola study may be affected by strength, size, coordination, intelligence, rate of development, attitudes toward study, motivation for learning, ability to use time efficiently, and proficiency in practice skills. A deficiency in any of these areas could lead to musical stagnation.

The teacher, who is dealing with the process of change, must consider the various facets of the individual if he is to guide the student's growth in directions that are pedagogically sound. At the teacher's command are observable characteristics, mannerisms, habits, proven ability, suspected latent talents, apparent drive, and traits of temperament. Through observation of the student at his lesson, the teacher may secure useful information about the efficiency of his practice habits, his rate of comprehension, the degree of control of his movements, and his tenacity and resourcefulness. Many teachers fail to recognize that not all students learn in the same way. Whether the student learns better aurally, visually, mentally, or tactilely is not so important as the fact that the teacher recognizes these special abilities and puts them to good use in the learning process. Observation of the individual as he learns new material may yield clues as to whether his learning is channeled primarily through the eye, the ear, the mind, or the fingers and may indicate weak areas that need remedial work.

The basic characteristics and special needs of each individual student must be known before the teacher can help set appropriate levels of aspiration. Frequently the precise meaning of achievement is not clear to the student. Periodic examination of student progress should be made and these findings shared with the student, even to the extent of sending an evaluation home to the parent.

A large part of a teacher's time is devoted to five areas:

Setting up a program of instruction for each individual student
Training the student to be independent in problem solving
Evaluating the student's progress toward desirable objectives
Identifying factors that are interfering with the student's progress
Modifying the teaching-learning process in order to assure greater and more rapid progress

Finding the correct sequence of learning activities is one of the major problems an inexperienced teacher must face. Since learning is a step-by-step process, a step overlooked or only partly learned leads to a slowing down in the rate of learning. A careful study of some common errors in teaching may save the viola teacher many mistakes in judgment.

Common Errors in Teaching

Ignoring individual differences
Letting expectations exceed the student's ability

Failing to ascertain readiness at all stages of development

Failing to correct specific difficulties before moving on to more complex tasks

Early teaching inadequate for later development

Lack of stress on comprehension

Failing to develop adequate concepts and perception of relationships

Not emphasizing need for efficient practice habits

Not using a multi-sensory approach

Not stressing achievement, goals and rewards

Insufficient remedial drill

Not relating drills to specific musical examples

Teaching compositions instead of principles of performance

Being overly analytical, particularly with younger students

Putting too much emphasis on speed at early stage of development

No genuine interest in teaching or in creating warm relationships with students

Failure to notice deficiencies in kinesthesia, sight, or aural acuity

Use of music improperly chosen for developmental level (poor grading)

Lack of variety of material at any stage of development

Sparsity of material leading to excessive repetition and eventual disinterest

Problem Solving

The modern pedagogue must face the fact that the student is not equipped with the proper analytical skills needed to respond adequately to musical materials or to pursue a course of self-correction. The building of playing techniques revolves around solving problems from the simple to the complex. Seldom is the individual aware of all the considering, discarding, modifying, and analyzing that he does when he solves a problem. In an area so complex as musical performance, whole series of problems face the player. For the viola student, problems must be separated into component parts and the components analyzed separately.

Steps in Problem Solving

Selection of a problem

Recognition of the need for solving the problem

Instruction in proper technique for solving the problem

Selection of pertinent information for the solution

Initial response

Detections of errors in response

Redirection and attempted correction

Improved response

Perception of improvement

Reinforcement through repetition
Recognition of progress

While the above steps in problem solving may appear to be more applicable to scientific inquiry than to musical performance, they are a product of the author's own experience in improving instrumental performance and apply to all levels of instruction. When applied to the instrumental techniques listed in Chapter II, improved performance should take place.

Failure in problem solving occurs for several reasons. The problem may be inadequately defined or it may be circumvented altogether. Failure may result from refusing to explore more than one approach to a solution. In seeking a quick solution, essential elements may be overlooked. The acceptance of imperfect solutions will impede progress.

CONCLUSION

String players may reach professional status through completely different materials and teaching methods. Since individuals have varying abilities, interests, needs, rates of learning, and degrees of motivation, no set program of instruction would be adequate for all. Specific principles of teaching may be cited, however, that offer guidance and yet are non-restrictive.

Create a positive atmosphere that will call forth positive responses
Emphasize desirable patterns instead of defects
Impress on the student the need for concentration
Help the student form mental pictures of desired results
Attempt to solve only one problem at a time
Seek out, isolate, and remedy the small obstacles in performance
Vary daily routine and teaching approach to avoid boredom and fatigue
Look for new ideas to incorporate in teaching
Work toward perfecting one's own performing technique
Strive to increase one's own powers of observation and analysis

As teachers we are interested in the direction of a student's effort toward self-actualization and the realization of his potential. Smith and Dechant list as the motives that generally activate human behavior: "Self-esteem, self-realization, curiosity, security, and a need to be adequate, successful, and to belong. . . ."[9] Each of these needs can be satisfied by successful instrumental performance.

[9]Henry P. Smith and Emerald V. Dechant, *Psychology in Teaching Reading* (Englewood Cliffs: Prentice Hall, Inc., 1961), p. 271.

Appendix

VIOLA MUSIC IN PRINT

I STUDY MATERIAL

SCHOOLS AND METHODS

Composer	Title	Editor	Publisher
Alessandri, Giuseppe	Esercizi e Letture ad uso dei candidati all esame di 8 anno di violino		Ricordi ER 1837
Amicabile	Viola Technique, 64 exercises for perfection		Bongiovanni
Applebaum, Samuel	String Builder 3 vol. Second and Fourth Position String Builder Third and Fifth Position String Builder (string class methods)		Belwin Belwin Belwin
Berger, Melvin	Basic Viola Technique		MCA
Bergh, Harris	String Positions (string class method)		Summy-Birchard
Bleier, Paul (1898-)	Violaschule		Hieber
Bornoff, George	Finger Patterns Fun for Fiddle Fingers Patterns in Position String Reader (string class methods)		Thompson Thompson Thompson CF 04592
Brown, James	Polychordia String Tutor 12 vol.		STB
Brown, Hullah	Bow-Craft Viola Tutor		Williams
Bruni, Antonio Bartolomeo (1751-1821)	Method and 25 Studies Method "School for Viola" Method "Viola Schule"	Borisovsky	Ricordi ER 90 MZK (MCA No. 2347) Schott
Brunner, Adolf (1901-)	Method for Viola		ZM (Pet No. ZM 3163)
Carse, Adam (1878-1958)	Viola School 5 vol.		Augener
Cavallini, Eugenio	Elementary and Progressive School 2 vol.		Ricordi ER122
Cheyette and Salzman	Beginning String Musicianship Intermediate String Musicianship (string class method)		Bourne Bourne
Consolini	Fundamental Principles		Bongiovanni 598
Copperwheat, Winifred	First Year Viola Method		Paxton
Dancla, Charles (1817-1907)	School of Mechanism, op. 74	Vieland	International
Dawe, Margery (1907-)	New Road to String Playing 3 vol. (string class method)		Cramer
Dilmore, Hermon	Breeze-Easy Method for Strings 2 vol. (string class method)		MPH
Edwards, Arthur	String Ensemble Method for Teacher Education (string class method)		Brown

SCHOOLS AND METHODS (Cont'd)

Composer	Title	Editor	Publisher
Etling, Forest	Solo Time for Strings (string class method)		Etling
——	Fay String Method		Paragon
Feldman, Harry	Unison String Class Method		Pro Art
Fischel and Bennett	Gambles Class Method for Strings 3 vol.		MPH
Gebauer, Michael Joseph (1763-1812)	Méthode		Lemoine
Ginot, Etienne	New Method of Initiation to Viola		Jobert
Gordon, Philip (1894-)	String Debut (string class method)		SB
Gordon, Beckstead, Stone	Visual Method for Strings		Highland
Green, Elizabeth	Hohmann for the String Class		CF
Herfurth, C. Paul	Tune a Day 2 vol. (string class method)		BMC
Herman, Helen	Bow and Strings 3 vol. (string class method)		Belwin
Hudadoff, Igor	Rhythm a Day (string class method)		Pro Art
Hyksa, Antonin	Technická cvičení v polohách II		Artia
	Technická cvičení pro violu III		Artia
Isaac, Merle (1898-)	Method 2 vol.		Cole
	String Method 2 vol. (string class methods)		Mel Bay
Johnson, Harold	Fillmore Beginning String Class		Fillmore
	Position for All Strings (string class methods)		FitzSimons
Jones, Dasch and Krone	Strings from the Start Part I		CF 02536
Jones, Edwin	Strings from the Start Part II (strings class methods)		CF
Keller and Taylor	Easy Steps to the Orchestra 2 vol. (string class method)		Mills
Klotman, Robert	Action with Strings (string class method)		Southern, Texas
Langey, Otto (1851-1922)	Celebrated Tutor		CF 0735
Laoureux-Iotti	Practical Method		GS 43460
Larsen, Hans	Bratsch skole		Hansen
Laubach, Alfred	Practical Viola School		Augener
Lewis	Method		Cole
Mackay, Neil (1924-)	Modern Viola Method		Oxford
Mackenzie, Clemewell	Play Right Away (string class method)		Pro Art
Maddy, Joseph (1891-1966)	Symphonic String Course (string class method)		Kjos
Martin, Pauline	Funway to Fiddletown		Pro Art
	Runway to Fiddletown (string class methods)		Pro Art
Martinn	Méthode d Alto	Laforge	Billaudot
Matesky and Womeck	Learning to Play a Stringed Instrument		Prentice-Hall

Composer	Title	Editor	Publisher
Michelini, Bruto	Scuolo della viola		Ricordi ER2466
Moehlmann and Skornicka	Boosey and Hawkes Instrumental Course for Strings (string class method)		BH
Mollier, Leon	Nouvelle Méthode d Alto 2 vol.		Salabert
Morrison	String Class System		Presser
Müller and Rusch	String Method 5 vol.		Kjos
Naumann, Georg	Volkstümliche Bratschenschule		Hofmeister
Orszagh, Tivadar	Viola Tutor		Kultura
Pascal, Léon (1899-)	Technique de l Alto		Eschig
Pernecky, Jack	Growing with Strings (string class method)		Cole
Preston, Herbert	Direct Approach to Higher Positions (string class method)		Belwin
Sabatini, Renzo (1905-)	Metodo Practico per Viola		Carisch
Schradieck, Henry (1846-1918)	School of Viola Technique 3 vol.	Pagels	International
	School of Viola Technique 3 vol.		Cranz
	School of Viola Technique Book 1	Lifschey	GS L1750
Ševčik, Otakar (1852-1934)	School of Technic, op. 1, 3 vol.	Tertis	Bosworth
	School of Technic, op. 1, Part 1	Aronoff	EV
Sitt, Hans (1850-1922)	Method	Ambrosio	CF 0362
	Method		International
	Method "Viola School"		Peters 2588
Spindler, Fritz	Bausteine zur Entwicklung einer virtuosen Violatechnik 2 vol.		Pro Musica 147-148
Szaleski	Viola Course		PWM
Tours, Berthold (1838-1897)	The Viola	Shore	Novello
Vashaw and Smith	Work and Play String Method 2 vol.		Presser
Volmer, Berta (1908-)	Bratschenschule 2 vol.		Schott 4613-4614
Waller, Gilbert	String Class Method 2 vol.		Kjos
	Vibrato Method		Kjos
Wesseley, Hans (1862-1926)	Practical School 2 vol.		Williams 04216-04217
Whistler and Nord	Beginning Strings (string class method)		CF
Wikstrom, Thomas	Techniques for Strings (string class method)		CF
Wunderlich, Helen	String Class Method		Oxford
Zerbe and Zerbe	String-Art Class Method		Markert
Zwissler, Ruth	First Lessons for Beginning Strings (string class method)		Highland

CAPRICES, STUDIES, EXERCISES

Alessandri	Sight Reading Exercises		Ricordi ER1837
Anzoletti, Marco	12 Studies		Ricordi ER121
Applebaum, Samuel	Early Etudes for Strings		Belwin

CAPRICES, STUDIES, EXERCISES (Cont'd)

Composer	Title	Editor	Publisher
Blumenstengel, Albrecht	24 Studies, op. 33	Wiemann	International 1549
Brown, James	Drills for Violin and Viola Players		STB
Bruni, Antonio Bartolomeo (1751-1821)	25 Studies	Ambrosio	CF 03319
	25 Studies	Schulz	International 1373
Campagnoli, Bartolommeo (1751-1827)	41 Caprices, op. 22	Consolini	Ricordi ER114
	41 Caprices	Kreuz	Augener 7651
	41 Caprices	Lifschey	GS L1676
	41 Caprices	Primrose	International 1627
	41 Caprices		Peters 2548
	24 Caprices, op. 22	Schmidtner	Sikorski 317
	7 Divertimenti, op. 18	Spindler	Hofmeister
Casimir	24 Preludes in all keys	Ney	Ed M
Cocchia	Esercizi sulle doppie corde in prima posizione		Curci
Courte, Robert	Daily Technical Exercises		UMP
Dancla, Charles (1817-1907)	14 Etudes, op. 68, for two violas		Peters 9090
Dont, Jacob (1815-1888)	20 Progressive Exercises, op. 38	Svecenski	GS L1493
	Etüden und Capricen, op. 35	Rostal	Schott 6118
	Studies, op. 35	Spindler	Hofmeister
	Studies, op. 37	Spindler	Hofmeister
	24 Studies, op. 37	Vieland	International
Dounis, Demetrius (1886-1954)	Specific Technical Exercises, op. 23		CF B2605
Fiorillo, Federigo (1755- ?)	36 Etüden-Capricen	Spindler	Hofmeister
	31 Selected Studies	Pagels	International 970
Fischer, Bernard	Selected Studies and Etudes		Belwin E.L.487
Forbes, Watson (1909-)	Book of Daily Exercises		Oxford 22.005
	Exercises for Viola Players 4 vol.		ABRSM
Frank, Marco (1881-)	Viola Etudes 3 vol.		OBV
Fuchs, Lillian (1903-)	15 Characteristic Studies		Oxford 92.202
	16 Fantasy Etudes		FC 2088
Gaviniès, Pierre (1728-1800)	24 Matinées	Abbado	Ricordi ER 2556
	Studies	Spitzner	International
Gifford, Alexander	12 Studies in the First, Second and Third Positions		Augener
Göring, Louis	6 Übungen		Hofmeister
Green, Elizabeth	12 Modern Etudes for the Advanced Violist		EV
Hermann, Friedrich	6 Concert Studies, op. 18		International
	Technical Studies, op. 22		International
Hoffmeister, Franz Anton (1754-1812)	12 Etudes	Hermann	International 785
	12 Etudes	Schmidtner	Sikorski 329
	12 Etudes		Peters 1993

Composer	Title	Editor	Publisher
Hofmann, Richard (1844-1918)	First Studies, op. 86 First Studies 15 Studies, op. 87		International 432 Peters 2732 International
Jentsch, Walter (1900-)	3 Studies, op. 36		Sikorski 667
Kayser, Heinrich (1815-1888)	Studies, op. 20 Studies 36 Studies, op. 43	Lesinsky Vieland	CF 03824 International International 883
Kinsey, Herbert	Easy Progressive Studies for Viola 2 vol.		ABRSM
Kreutzer, Rodolphe (1766-1831)	42 Studies 42 Studies 42 Studies	Blumenau Consolini Pagels	GS L1737 Ricordi ER117 International
Kreuz, Emil (1867-1932)	Progressive Studies, op. 40 4 vol. Select Studies 5 vol.		Augener 7653 a,b,c,d Augener 7657 a,b,c,d,e
Lehmann	Studien für Viola (1966)		Schott
Lifschey, Samuel	Daily Technical Studies Double-Stop Studies		CF GS
Massias, Gérard (1933-)	12 Etudes		Jobert
Matz, Arnold (1904-)	25 Capricen Intonation Studies 5 vol. 7 Studies, second position in all keys 8 Studies, third position in all keys		Hofmeister BRH Peters 5386 Peters 5387
Mazas, Jacques-Féréol (1782-1849)	Études Spéciales, op. 36 Book 1 Études Brilliantes, op. 36 Book 2	Pagels Pagels	International 1091 International 428
Mogill	Selected Etudes		Elkan
Moravec, Karel	Selected Studies 3 vol.		Artia
— —	28 Etudes for Strings (DeBeriot, Kayser, Sitt, Wohlfahrt)	Müller	Belwin

ORCHESTRAL STUDIES

	Orchestral Difficulties from the Works of Tchaikowsky	Strakhov	MZK
	Orchestral Excerpts from Classical and Modern Works 3 vol.	Vieland	International
	Orchestral Excerpts from the Works of Johannes Brahms	Lifschey	AMP
	Orchestral Studies 6 vol.		Hofmeister
	Orchestral Studies: Richard Strauss	Steiner	Peters 4189c
	Orchestral Studies: Richard Strauss		International
	Orchestral Studies: Richard Wagner	Unkenstein	BRH
	Orchestral Studies: Richard Wagner		International
Paganini, Niccolò (1782-1840)	24 Caprices, op. 1 6 Caprices, op. 1		International Ricordi ER2526
Palaschko, Johannes	10 Artists Etudes op. 44 10 Concert Etudes 24 Études mélodigues, op. 77 20 Studies, op. 36 12 Studies, op. 62		ZM 1731 MZK Leduc International 905 Ricordi ER292
Pascal, Léon (1899-)	25 Divertissements		Heugel

CAPRICES, STUDIES, EXERCISES (Cont'd)

Composer	Title	Editor	Publisher
Polo, Enrico (1868-1953)	Studi di tecnica		Ricordi ER 2003
Primrose, William (1903-)	Technique Is Memory		Oxford 29.004
Reese	22 Studies (from Wohlfahrt, Hofmann, Henning)		Belwin
Rode, Pierre (1774-1830)	24 Caprices	Blumenau	GS L1736
	24 Caprices	Hoenisch	Peters 4861
	24 Caprices	Pagels	International 790
	24 Caprices	Spindler	Hofmeister
Rolla, Alessandro (1757-1841)	Esercizio ed Arpeggio		EdM
Rovelli, Pietro (1793-1838)	12 Caprices	Pagels	International 1372
	12 Caprices	Spindler	Hofmeister
Sauzay, Eugène (1809-1901)	Etudes harmoniques	Laforge	Billaudot
Schloming, Harry	24 Studies, op. 15		Simrock
Schmidtner, Franz (1913-)	Daily Studies		Sikorski 451
Ševčik, Otakar (1852-1934)	Selected Studies in the First Position, op. 1	Lifschey	GS L1739
Sitt, Hans (1850-1922)	15 Etudes, op. 116		Eulenberg (Pet No. ES 198)
Ticciati, Niso (1924-)	10 Exercises for String Ensemble		Oxford 29.003
Vaughan Williams, Ralph (1872-1958)	6 Studies in English Folk Song		STB
Vieux, Maurice (1884-)	20 Études		Leduc
	10 Études sur des traits d'orchestre		Leduc
	10 Études sur les intervalles		Leduc
Volmer, Berta (1908-)	Etüden		Schott 4688
Whistler, Harvey	Essential Exercises and Etudes		Rubank
Wohlfahrt, Franz	Foundation Studies 2 vol.		CF 02659-02660
	30 Studies 2 vol.	Vieland	International

DOUBLE-STOPS

Cocchia	Esercizi sulle doppie corde in prima posigione		Curci
Lifschey, Samuel	Double-Stop Studies		GS
Schradieck, Henry (1846-1918)	School of Viola Technique, Vol. 2	Pagels	International Cranz

SCALES AND ARPEGGIOS

Applebaum, Samuel	Scales for Strings 2 vol. (string class method)		Belwin
Berger, Melvin	Basic Viola Technique		MCA
Cooley, Carlton	Scales and Arpeggios		Elkan

Composer	Title	Editor	Publisher
Flesch, Carl (1873-1944)	Scale System	Karman	CF 02921
Forbes, Watson (1909-)	Book of Scales and Arpeggios 3 vol.		Oxford 22.034, 22.812, 22.807
Kreuz, Emil (1867-1932	Scales and Arpeggios 2 vol.		Augener
Laforge	Gammes journalières et arpèges		Billaudot
Lifschey, Samuel	Scale and Arpeggio Studies 2 vol.		GS
Primrose, William (1903-)	Art and Practice of Scale Playing on the Viola		Mills
Ševčik, Otakar (1852-1934)	Changes of Position and Preparatory Scale Studies, op. 8	Aronoff	EV
	Changes of Position and Preparatory Scale Studies, op. 8	Tertis	Bosworth
Schinina, Luigi	Scale e Arpeggi		Curci
Vaksman, A.	Scales and Exercises		MZK (MCA No. 2348)
Whistler and Hummel	Elementary Scales and Bowing		Rubank
	Intermediate Scales and Bowing (string class methods)		Rubank 1451-15

SHIFTING

Composer	Title	Editor	Publisher
Applebaum, Samuel	Second and Fourth Position String Builder		Belwin
	Third and Fifth Position String Builder (string class methods)		
Best, George	Early String Shifting (string class method)		Varitone
Bornoff, George	Patterns in Position (string class method)		Thompson
Gifford, Alexander	12 Studies in the First, Second and Third Position		Augener
Johnson, Harold	Positions for All Strings (string class method)		Varitone
Lukacs, Pal	Exercises in Change of Position		Kultura
Mackay, Neil (1924-)	Position Changing for Viola		Oxford 22.039
Preston, Herbert	Direct Approach to Higher Positions (string class method)		Belwin
Ševčik, Otakar (1852-1934)	Changes of Position and Preparatory Scale Studies, op. 8	Aronoff	EV
	Changes of Position and Preparatory Scale Studies	Tertis	Bosworth 21509
Whistler, Harvey (1907-)	Introducing the Positions 2 vol.		Rubank

II SOLO PIECES

VIOLA ALONE

Composer	Title	Editor	Publisher
Angerer, Paul (1927-)	Musik		Doblinger
Arel, Bülent (1918-)	Music for Viola		Impero

VIOLA ALONE (Cont'd)

Composer	Title	Editor	Publisher
Arnell, Richard (1917-)	Partita	Forbes	Hinrichsen (Pet No. H721)
Bach, Johann Sebastian (1685-1750)	Chaconne	Tertis	Augener 5568
	Fantasia Cromatica	Kodaly-Primrose	BH 17875
	Siciliano	Cazden	Spratt
	Six Sonatas and Partitas 3 vol. (originally for violin)	Forbes	Peters 7035AbC
	Six Sonatas and Partitas	Polo	Ricordi ER2208
	Six Sonatas and Partitas	— —	Ricordi ER2208
	Six Sonatas and Partitas	Spindler	Hofmeister
	Six Suites (originally for violoncello)	Boulay	Leduc
	Six Suites	Giuranna	Ricordi ER2267
	Six Suites	Forbes	Chester
	Six Suites	Lifschey	GS L1564
	Six Suites	Polo	Ricordi ER1022
	Six Suites	Markevitch	Presser
	Six Suites	Spindler	Hofmeister
	Six Suites	Svecenski	GS L1278
	Six Suites	Schmidtner	Sikorski 316
— —	3 Fourteenth-Century Dances (optional Tambour)	Berger	MCA
Beyer	Cadenzas to Viola Concertos by Hoffmeister, K. Stamitz, Zelter		Peters GM22
Biber, Heinrich (1644-1704)	Passacaglia (originally for violin)	Rostal	Chester
Bandini, Bruno	Prelude		Ricordi BA6283
Bloch, Ernest (1880-1959)	Suite		Broude
Brün, Herbert (1918-)	Sonatina		IMP
Brunswick, Mark (1902-)	Fantasia		Valley
Burkhard, Willy (1900-1955)	Sonate, op. 59		Bärenreiter 2094
Cazden, Norman (1914-)	Chamber Sonata, op. 17, no. 2		CFE
Cooley, Carlton	Etude Suite		Elkan
David, Johann (1895-)	Sonata, op. 31, no. 3		BRH
Duke, John (1899-)	Suite		Valley
Franco, Johan (1908-)	Sonata		CFE
Fuchs, Lillian (1903-)	Sonata Pastorale		AMP 95519
Geier, Oskar	Suite		Hofmeister
Genzmer, Harald (1909-)	Sonata		Peters 5860

Composer	Title	Editor	Publisher
Gibbons, Orlando (1583-1625)	6 Fantasias, 2 vol.	Mueller	Noetzel (Pet No. N1268-9)
Grainger, Percy (1882-1961)	Arrival Platform, Room Music no. 7		Schott
Gross, Robert	Sonatina		CFE
Hampe, Charlotte (1910-)	7 Short Baroque Dances		RE (Pet No. RE5)
Hindemith, Paul (1895-1963)	Sonata, op. 11, no. 5 Sonata, op. 25, no. 1		Schott Schott
Hoessl, Albert	Suite		Cor ST5
Hovhaness, Alan (1911-)	Chahagir, op. 56a		Broude
Hueber, Kurt (1928-)	Sonata, op. 4		Noetzel (Pet No. N6141)
Jemnitz, Alexander (1890-1963	Sonata, op. 46		Kultura
Kaminski, Heinrich (1886-1946)	Prelude and Fugue		Peters 4446
Krenek, Ernst (1900-)	Sonata, op. 92, no. 3		Bomart
Kurtág, György (1926-)	Signes, op. 5		Kultura
Lakner, Yehoshua (1924-)	Improvisation		IMP
Lehmann, Hans (1937-)	Studien		Schott
Levitin, Yuri (1912-)	Variations		MZK 2351
Levy, Frank	Sonata		Cor ST1
Luening, Otto (1900-)	Sonata		CFE
Lutyens, Elizabeth (1906-)	Sonata, op. 5, no. 4		Lengnick
Marcel, Luc-André (1919-)	Sonata		Transatlantiques
Orgad, Ben (1926-)	Monologue		IMP
Paganini, Niccolò (1782-1840)	6 Caprices, op. 1 (originally for violin) 24 Caprices, op. 1 (originally for violin)	Ferraguzzi Raby	Ricordi International 405
Perle, George (1915-)	Sonata		ECIC
Polo, Enrico (1868-1953)	3 Studi-Sonate		SZ
Porter, Quincy (1897-1966)	Suite		Valley
Reger, Max (1873-1916)	3 Suites, op. 131 3 Suites		Peters 3971 International

VIOLA ALONE (Cont'd)

Composer	Title	Editor	Publisher
Reutter, Hermann (1900-)	Cinco Caprichos sobre Cervantes		Schott 6108
Rolla, Antonio (1798-1837)	6 Idylles		EdM
Scher, V.	Sonata	Kramarov	MZK (MCA No. 2280)
Schroeder, Hanning (1904-)	Music in 5 Movements		Lienau (Pet No. R58b)
Sehlbach, Erich (1898-)	Music for Viola Solo, op. 87, no. 1		Möseler
Serebrier, José (1938-)	Sonata		SMP
Shulman, Alan (1915-)	Suite		Templeton
Smith, Leland	Suite		CFE
Stearns, Peter	Variations		CFE
Stadlmair, Hans (1929-)	Sonata		BRH
Stravinsky, Igor (1882-)	Elegie		AMP
Telemann, Georg Philipp (1681-1767)	12 Fantasias 2 vol.	Rood	MM
Toch, Ernst (1887-1964)	3 Impromptus, op. 90		Mills 40170
Voss, Friedrich (1930-)	Variations		BRH
Vycpálek, Ladislav (1882-)	Suite, op. 21		Artia
Wellesz, Egon (1885-)	Rhapsody, op. 87		Doblinger
Wiener, Stéphane	Sonata in D		Choudens (Pet No. 6038)
Zimmermann, Bernd (1918-)	Sonata (1955)		Schott 5908
Zonn, Paul	Sonata		CFE

VIOLA AND PIANO

Adolphus, Milton	Improvisations, op. 61		CFE
Aguirre, Julián (1868-1924)	Huella	Heifetz-Primrose	CF B2672
Albeniz, Isaac (1860-1909)	Tango	Forbes	Oxford
Aletter, William	Mélodie		CF B2319
	Petite Gavotte		CF B2353
Amirov, Fikret- (1922-)	Elegy	Anshelevich	MZK (MCA No. 2281)

Composer	Title	Editor	Publisher
Amram, David (1930-)	Wind and the Rain		Peters 6692
Anderson, Kenneth (1903-)	3 Diversions		Bosworth
Ashton, A.	Landler		STB
	Tarantella		STB
Avshalomov, Jacob (1919-)	Evocations		CFE
Babbitt, Milton (1916-)	Compositions		Bomart
Bach, Johann Christoph (1642-1703)	Lament		EdM
Bach, Johann Sebastian (1685-1750)	Adagio	Borissovsky	International
	Adagio	Grant	Concert
	Adagio	Siloti-Tertis	CF B1950
	Air	Wilhelmj-Pagels	CF B2468
	Air and Gavotte	Ries	Schott
	Air and Gavottes	Tolhurst	Williams
	Air from Christmas Oratorio	Alexanian	Salabert
	All glory be to God on high	Forbes-Richardson	Oxford 22.020
	Andante		Curwen
	Andante	Ronchini	Eschig
	Arioso	Isaac	CF B2496
	Bourree	Browne	Williams (Mil No. W1406)
	Come, Redeemer of our race	Forbes-Richardson	Oxford 22.102
	Gavotte in A	Forbes	Oxford 22.330
	It is finished	Krane	Spratt
	Komm', süsser Tod	Tertis	GS
	Largo, dalla Cantata "Gottes Zeit ist die allerbeste Zeit"	Janigro	Ricordi 127917
	Lord, Jesus Christ, be present now	Forbes-Richardson	Oxford 22.021
	3 Pieces from Sonata No. 1	Johnson	Lengnick (Mil No. L2006)
	Praeludium	Shore	BH
	Prelude in A	Forbes	Oxford 22.320
	Prelude and Gigue	Cooley	MCA
	Sheep may safely graze	Forbes	Oxford 23.416
	Siciliano	Cazden	Spratt
Bach, Karl Philipp Emanuel (1714-1788)	Solfegietto	Primrose	CF B2683
Bacich, Anthony	Tone Poems		Willis
Bacon, Ernst (1898-)	Koschatiana		MCA
Badings, Henk (1907-)	Cavatina		Donemus (Pet No. D7)
Baervoets	Rhapsody		Metropolis

VIOLA AND PIANO (Cont'd)

Composer	Title	Editor	Publisher
Baklanova, N.	Russian Folk Song—Spinning Wheel		MZK (MCA No. 2285)
Barati, George (1913-)	Cantabile e Ritmico		Peer
Barlow, David	Siciliano		Novello
Barnett, David	Ballade, op. 16	Primrose	Oxford 92.201
Bartók, Béla (1881-1945)	Evening in the Village	Vaczy	Kultura
Bazelaire, Paul (1886-1958)	Funerailles, op. 120		Salabert
Beale, James (1924-)	Ballade, op. 23		CFE
Beethoven, Ludwig van (1770-1827)	Alla Polacca	Forbes	Oxford 22.033
	Country Dances	Forbes-Richardson	Oxford 22.004
	Menuetto from Sonata in E flat, op. 31	Jacobson	Cramer
	7 Mozart Variations	Forbes-Richardson	Peters 7049
	Notturno, op. 42	Beck	GS 41948
	Notturno	Primrose	Schott 10091
	Romance in F	Kreuz	Augener
	2 Romances	Hermann	Peters 2413
	2 Romances		International 1243
	Rondo	Forbes	Schott 10562
	Variations on a Theme of Mozart	Tertis	BH 7557
Ben-Haim, Paul (1897-)	3 Songs Without Words		IMP
Benjamin, Arthur (1893-1960	Le Tombeau de Ravel		BH 18432
	From San Domingo	Primrose	BH
	Jamaican Rumba	Primrose	BH
Bergsma, William (1921-)	Fantastic Variations		Galaxy 2240
Beriot, Charles de 1802-1870)	Serenade	Applebaum	Belwin
Bezrukov, G.	3 Easy Pieces		MZK (MCA No. 2286)
Bigot, Eugene (1885-1965)	Thême et variations		Durand
Bizet, Georges (1838-1875)	Adagietto aus L'Arlésienne Suite	Primrose	Schott 10415
	Aria aus L'Arlésienne Suite		Choudens 259
Bloch, Ernest (1880-1959)	Meditation and Processional		GS 43028
Bohm, Carl	Perpetual Motion from Third Suite, No. 6	Isaac-Lewis	CF B1385
Boisdeffre, René de (1836-1906)	3 Pièces		Hamelle
Boni, P.	Largo and Allegro	Lepilov	MZK (MCA No. 2287)
Borodin, Alexander (1833-1887)	Nocturne (originally for string quartet)	Primrose	Oxford 22.031
	Scherzo (originally for string quartet)	Primrose	Oxford 22.032

Composer	Title	Editor	Publisher
Borodkin	Synco-Rhythmicon		MPH
Bournonville, Armand	Appassionata		Billaudot
Boyce, William (1710-1779)	Tempo di gavotta	Craxton-Forbes	Oxford 20.108
Braein, Edvard (1887-1957)	Serenade		Lyche (Pet No. LY4)
Brahms, Johannes (1833-1897)	Hungarian Dances, no. 1 and no. 3	Forbes	Hinrichsen (Pet. No. H699)
	Waltz, op. 39, no. 2	Grunes	Omega
	Wie Melodien zieht es mir, op. 105, no. 1	Primrose	CF B2680
Bréville, Pierre de (1861-1949)	Prière		RL
Britten, Benjamin (1913-)	Lachrymae, op. 48		BH
Brown	Caprice		Salabert
Brown, James	Air and English Jig		STB
	Burletta		STB
	Chauvre Souris		STB
	Fling		STB
	Pedlar		STB
	Promenade		STB
	Revellers		STB
	Rondeau en Musette		STB
	Sprigged Muslin		STB
	Tea-Time		STB
	Viola D'Amore Waltz		STB
Browne, P.	David of the Whiterock		Williams 04274
	Snowy Breasted Pearl		Williams 04281
Bruch, Max (1838-1920)	Romance, op. 85		Schott
Buchtel, Forrest (1899-)	Ambition Waltz		Kjos S-5100
	Happy Days		Kjos S-5103
	Jolly Fellows		Kjos S-5104
Bulakov, P.	Barcarolle		MZK
Bush, Alan (1900-)	Dance Melody, op. 47		Williams 1421
	Song Melody, op. 47		Williams 1420
Butterworth, Neil	2 French Pieces		Chappell
Caix-D'Hervelois, Louis de (c1680-c1760)	La Chambor, Allemande	Marchet	International
Caldara, Antonio (c1670-1736)	Canto	Rostal	Chester
Campagnoli, Bartolommeo (1751-1827)	Divertissements	Ginot	Jobert
Capitanio, Isidoro (1874-1942)	Leggenda in A		SZ
Carles, Marc (1933-)	Intensités		Leduc

119

VIOLA AND PIANO (Cont'd)

Composer	Title	Editor	Publisher
Carse, Adam (1878-1958)	Breezy Story		Augener
	Calm Reflections		Augener
	Heartache		Augener
	Thoughtfulness		Augener
Carter, Elliott (1908-)	Elegy		SMP
	Pastoral		Presser
Cazden, Norman (1914-)	3 Recitations, op. 24		CFE
Cece, Alfredo	Recitativo		Zanibon (Pet No. ZA4785)
Challan, Henri (1910-)	Diptyque		Leduc
Chausson, Ernest (1855-1899)	Pièce, op. 39		Salabert
	Interlude		International 664
Chaynes, Charles	Alternances		Leduc
Chopin, Frédéric (1810-1849)	Nocturne in E flat, op. 9, no. 2	Sarasate-Rehfeld	CF B1386
Cirri, Giambattista (1724-1808)	Arioso		EdM
Clarke, Henry (1907-)	Nocturne		CFE
Clarke, Rebecca (1886-)	Passacaglia on an old English tune		GS 40192
Cocchia	Moto perpetuo		Forlivesi 12320
Cooley, Carlton	Song and Dance		Senart
Cools, Eugène (1877-1936)	Andante serio		Eschig
	Berceuse, op. 86		Eschig
	Poème, op. 74		Eschig
Corelli, Arcangelo (1653-1713)	Prelude and Allemande	Akon	Mills
Cortese, Luigi (1899-)	Improviso, op. 46		Curci
Cowell, Henry (1897-1965)	Hymn and Fuguing Tune no. 7		Peer
Creston, Paul (1906-)	Homage		GS
Cruft, Adrian (1921-)	Impromptu in B flat, op. 22		Williams
	Romance, op. 13		Williams
Cui, César (1835-1918)	Orientale	Gottlieb-Saenger	CF B1387
Dare, Marie	Le Lac		Chester
Dargomizhsky, Alexander (1813-1869)	Elegy	Borisovsky	MZK (MCA No. 2290)
Davidov, Karl (1838-1889)	Romance		MZK (MCA No. 2291)

Composer	Title	Editor	Publisher
Debussy, Claude (1862-1918)	Beau Soir	Katims	International
	Clair de Lune	Cazden	Spratt
	Il pleure dans mon coeur	Hartmann	EdM
	Romance	Katims	International
Decadt, J.	Nocturne		Metropolis
Delius, Frederick (1862-1934)	Serenade from Hassan	Tertis	BH
DiBiase, Edoardo	Reverie		CF B2978
DiDonato, Anthony	Variations on a Theme of Schumann		Bongiovanni 1214a
Dinicu, Grigoras (1889-1949)	Hora Staccato	Heifetz-Primrose	CF B2671
Dittersdorf, Karl Ditters von (1739-1799)	Andantino	Primrose	International
Dodgson, Stephen	4 Fancies		Chappell-L
Dressel, Erwin (1909-)	Partita		RE (Pet No. RE36)
Drigo, Richard (1846-1930)	Serenade	Schloming-Ambrosio	CF B1389
Duke, John (1899-)	Melody in E flat		EV
Dunhill, Thomas (1877-1946)	Alla Sarabande		Williams
	In Courtly Company		Williams
	Meditation on a study by Schumann		Williams
	Willow Brook		Williams
Duvernoy, Victor-Alphonse (1842-1907)	Lied		Hamelle
Dvarionas, Balis (1904-)	Theme and Variations	Lepilov	MZK (MCA No. 2292)
Dvořák, Antonín (1841-1904)	Bagatelle, op. 47, no. 3	Forbes	Hinrichsen (Pet No. H626b)
	Humoresque, op. 101, no. 7	Saenger-Himmel	CF B1390
Dyer, John	In Cheerful Mood		Williams 04286
	In Quiet Mood		Williams 04284
	In the Row		ABRSM 320
	In Whimsical Mood		Williams 04285
	Mantilla		Augener
	Meditation		Augener
	Old Redcoat		ABRSM 321
	On the Serpentine		ABRSM 322
	Tempo di Gavotta		ABRSM 323
	Woodland Serenade		Augener
Dyson, George (1883-1964)	Prelude, Fantasy and Chaconne		Novello
Edelson	Night Song		EdM
Edmunds, Christopher (1899-)	4 Pieces		Lengnick (Mil No. L2001)
	Windmill		Lengnick (Mil No. L2008)

121

VIOLA AND PIANO (Cont'd)

Composer	Title	Editor	Publisher
Elgar, Edward (1857-1934)	Canto Popolare (originally for orchestra)		Novello
	Pomp and Circumstance (originally for orchestra)	Akers	CF
	6 Very Easy Pieces, op. 22		Bosworth
Farkas, Ferenc (1905-)	Arioso		Kultura
	Rumanian Folk Dances		Kultura
Fauré, Gabriel (1845-1924)	Après un rêve (originally for voice)	Katims	International
	Elegy, op. 24 (originally for violoncello)	Katims	International
	Lamento (originally for voice)	Katims	International
	Sicilenne, op. 78 (originally for violoncello)	Katims	International
Ferguson, Howard (1908-)	4 Short Pieces		BH
Fibich, Zdenko (1850-1900)	Poem (originally for piano)	Ambrosio-Isaac-Lewis	CF B2375
Fitelberg, Jerzy (1903-1951)	Serenade		SMP
Forbes, Watson (1909-)	Scottish Tunes	Richardson	Oxford 22.806
Forst, Rudolf (1900-)	Homage to Ravel		EdM
Fortino, Mario	Prelude and Rondo		Tritone
Foster, Stephen (1826-1864)	Jeanie with the Light Brown Hair	Heifetz-Primrose	CF B2672
Franck, Maurice (1892-)	Theme et Variation		Durand
Franklin, Howard	Moonlight on the River		CF B2320
Freed, Isadore (1900-1960)	Rhapsody		CF B2706
Friskin, James (1886-)	Elegy		STB
Fuleihan, Anis (1900-)	Recitative and Sicilienne		GS
Gadzhibekov, Uzeir (1885-1948)	Azerbaijan Folk Song		MZK
Galuppi, Baldassare (1706-1785)	Aria amorosa	Tertis	Augener
Gardner, Samuel (1891-)	From the Canebrake, op. 5, no. 1		GS
Gaubert, Philippe (1879-1941)	Ballade		Eschig
Ghent, Emmanuel (1925-)	Entelechy		Oxford 92.203
Giampieri, Alamiro	Fantasia		Ricordi ER 2038
Gifford, Alexander	Madrigal		Augener
Gipps, Ruth (1921-)	Lyric Fantasy		Fox

Composer	Title	Editor	Publisher
Glazunov, Alexander (1865-1936)	Elegie, op. 44		Belaieff (Pet No. Bel200)
	Elegie		International
	Serenade Espagnole	Ginot	Jobert
Glière, Reinhold (1875-1956)	Prelude; Romance; Rondo		MZK (MCA No. 22930)
Glinka, Mikhail (1804-1857)	Barcarolle	Borisovsky	MZK (MCA 2294)
	Children's Polka	Borisovsky	MZK (MCA 2295)
	Mazurka	Borisovsky	MZK (MCA 2296)
	Three Pieces		MZK (MCA 2297)
Gluck	4 Pieces		MZK
Gluck, Christoph (1714-1787)	O del mio dolce ardor	Elkan	Elkan
Godard, Benjamin (1849-1895)	Berceuse from Joceyln	Isaac-Lewis	CF B2428
Goedicke, Alexander (1877-1957)	Prelude		MZK (MCA No. 2298)
Golestan, Stan (1872-1956)	Arioso et Allegro de Concert		Salabert
Goltermann, Georg (1824-1898)	Andante from Concerto, op. 14		CF B2362
	Grand Duo, op. 15		Augener 7680b
Gossec, François-Joseph (1734-1829)	Gavotte	Isaac-Lewis	CF B2377
Gow, David (1924-)	Nocturne and Capriccio		Augener
Granados, Enrique (1867-1916)	Orientale, Spanish Dance no. 2	Katims	International
Grenz, Artur (1909-)	Fantasy, op. 12		Sikorski 191
Grieg, Edvard (1843-1907)	To the Spring	Forbes	Oxford
Grossman, Karl	Catilena		Concert
Grudzinski, Czeslaw	Miniatures	Gonet	PWM
Guerrini, Guido (1890-1965)	Arcadica (originally for oboe)		Curci
	Aria di Ciociaria		Bongiovanni 1026
Haertel	Evening Serenade	Tobani	CF B1394
Hamblen, Bernard (1877-1962)	Reverie		BH
Handel, Georg Friedrich (1685-1759)	3 Movements from Water Music Suite	Sontag	SB
	Preludium	Sontag	SB
	Largo		Augener
Hanesyan, Harutyun	Andantino		Eschig
	Prelude and Capriccio		Eschig
	Romance		Eschig
Harris, Roy (1898-)	Soliloquy and Dance		GS 39095
Harrison, Pamela (1915-)	Lament		Galliard
Hasse, J.	Bouree and Minuet		MZK (MCA No. 2300)

123

VIOLA AND PIANO (Cont'd)

Composer	Title	Editor	Publisher
Haubiel, Charles (1892-)	Lullaby		CP
Hauser, Miska (1822-1887)	Berceuse	Ambrosio-Isaac-Lewis	CF B2376
Haydn, Joseph (1732-1809)	Adagio (originally for string quartet)	Forbes	Oxford 20.106
	Air		Augener 10599
Herbert, Victor	Gypsy Love Song	Schoenfeld	MPH
	Romany Life	Schoenfeld	MPH
Hindemith, Paul (1895-1963	Meditation from Nobilissima Visione		Schott
Hively, Wells	Psalmody		CFE
Hoeffer	Viola Music (1946)		MT (Pet. No. MV1025)
Holland, Theodore (1878-1947)	Ellingham Marshes		Hinrichsen (Pet No. H340)
Holst, Imogene (1907-)	4 Easy Pieces		Augener
Honnoré, Leon	Moreceau de Concert		Gilles
Howard, John (1890-1964)	Still Waters		EdM
Humperdinck, Engelbert (1854-1921	Evening Prayer from Hansel and Gretel	Caruthers	BMC 13065
Huré Jean (1877-1930)	Petite Chanson		Salabert
Husa, Karel (1921-)	Poem		Schott 5283
Ibert, Jacques (1890-1962)	Aria		Leduc
d'Indy, Vincent (1851-1931	Lied, op. 19		International
Inghelbrecht, Désiré (1880-1965)	Impromptu		Leduc
	Nocturne		Salabert
	Prelude and Saltarello		Salabert
Ippolitov-Ivanov, Mikhail (1859-1935)	Piece		MZK
Jacob, Gordon (1895-)	Air and Dance		Oxford 22.408
	3 Pieces		Curwen
Jacobi, Frederick (1891-1952)	Fantasy		CF B2622
Jacobson, Maurice (1896-)	Berceuse		Oxford 22.023
	Humoreske		Lengnick
Jacoby, Hanoch (1909-)	King David's Lyre		IMP
Järnefelt, Armas (1869-1958)	Berceuse	Deery	CF B2351

Composer	Title	Editor	Publisher
Joachim, Joseph (1831-1907)	Hebrew Melodies, op. 9		Augener 7630
Jongen, Joseph (1873-1953)	Allegro appassionato		Leduc
Jullien, René	Lied, op. 36		Eschig
Kabalevsky, Dmitri (1904-)	Improvisations, op. 21, no. 1	Kievman	MCA
Kabalin, Fedor	Poems and Rhymes		Tritone
Kalinnikov, Vassili (1886-1901)	Chanson Triste Sad Song		EdM MZK (MCA No. 2303)
Kalliwoda, Johann (1801-1866)	6 Nocturnes, op. 186 3 Nocturnes, op. 186		Peters 2104 International
Kesnar	Americano Evening Campfire Festival Frolic		MPH MPH MPH
Ketelbey, Albert (1875-1959)	In a Monastery Garden	MacLean	MPH
Khandoshkin, Ivan (1747-1804)	Variations on a Russian Song		MZK
Kodaly, Zoltan (1882-1967)	Adagio		Kultura
Kompaneyetz	Poem-Monologue		MZK (MCA No. 2305)
Kornauth, Egon (1891-1959)	3 Pieces, op. 47		Doblinger
Krancher, W.	Rhapsody		Metropolis
Krol, Bernhard (1920-)	Lassus-Variationen, op. 33		Simrock
Kriukov, Vladimir (1902-)	2 Pieces, op. 13		MZK (MCA No. 2115)
Kukuck, Felicitas (1914-)	Fantasia		Möseler
Landau, Victor	Scherzo		CFE
Legley, Victor (1915-)	Elegiac Lied, op. 7 Spring Poem no. 2, op. 51		BCM BCM
Leighton, Kenneth (1929-)	Fantasia on the name BACH		Novello
Liadov, Anatol (1855-1914)	Prelude, op. 11, no. 1	Borisovsky	MZK (MCA No. 2307)
Liszt, Franz (1811-1886)	Liebesträum, Notturno no. 3 (originally for piano)	Tertis	Augener
	Romance Oubliée	Temesváry	Kultura
Lolivrel	Sérénade de Printemps		Eschig
-----	Londerry Air	Ambrosio-Isaac-Lewis	CF B2374
Lopez Buchardo, Carlos (1881-1948)	2 Piezas	Bandini	Ricordi-BA 6216
Lovell, Joan	4 Country Sketches		Augener 18691R

VIOLA AND PIANO (Cont'd)

Composer	Title	Editor	Publisher
Lvov, Alexey (1798-1870)	Folk Melody Caprice		MZK (MCA No. 2308)
MacDowell, Edward (1861-1908)	To a Wild Rose (originally for piano)	Isaac	CF B3321
	To a Wild Rose		Belwin
Maganini, Quinto (1897-)	Ancient Greek Meldoy		EdM
	Night Piece		EdM
	Song of a Chinese Fisherman		EdM
Marais, Marin (1656-1728)	Fantaisie	Boulay	Leduc
	5 Old French Dances	Aldis-Rowe	Chester
	Menuetto aus Pièces de viole, Bd. III		Hofmeister
Marteau, Henri (1874-1934)	Chaconne, op. 8		Simrock
Martelli, Henri	Concert Piece		Ricordi-Paris R2178
Martini, Giambattista (1706-1784)	Celebrated Gavotte		Kjos S5107
Martino, Donald (1931-)	3 Dances, op. 23		CFE
Martucci, Giuseppi (1856-1909)	Canto d'Amore, op. 38, no. 3	Quaranta-d'Ambrosio	Ricordi 125327
Mascagni, Pietro (1863-1945)	Siciliana from Cavalleria Rusticana		CF B2355
	Siciliana	Painter	MPH
Massenet, Jules (1842-1912)	Elégie from Les Erynnies, op. 10	Deery	CF B2354
Massis, A	Poème		Billaudot
Matz, Arnold (1904-)	Mixolydian Sonatina		Peters 4608
	Theme and Variations	Baer	BRH
Maury, Lowndes	Song without words		Western
Mazellier, Jules	Nocturne et rondeau		Billaudot
Medtner, Nikolai (1880-1951)	Fairy Tale, op. 51, no. 3		ZM (Pet No. ZM247)
Mendelssohn, Felix (1809-1847)	Song without words, op. 109	Katims	International
	2 Songs without words	Forbes	Chester
Migot, Georges (1891-)	Estampie		Leduc
Mihály, András	Rhapsody		Kultura
Milford, Robin (1903-1959)	Air		Oxford 22.027
Milhaud, Darius (1892-)	La Bruxelloise		Heugel
	La Californienne		Heugel
	La Parisienne		Heugel
	Wisconsonian		Heugel
Miller	3 Miniatures		Hinricksen (Pet NO. H421)
Monasipov, A.	Romance		MZK (MCA No. 2311)
Monteux, Pierre (1875-1964)	Arabesque		Salabert
	Mélodie		Salabert

Composer	Title	Editor	Publisher
Moór, Emanuel (1863-1931)	Prelude, op. 123	Katims	International
Moore, John	Scottish Song		Oxford 20.110
Monasipov, A	Romance		MZK 5087
Moule-Evans, David (1905-)	Moto perpetuo		Williams (Mil No. W1402)
Mourant, Walter	Fantasy		CFE
Mozart, Wolfgang Amadeus (1756-1791)	Adagio and Rondo	Forbes-Richardson	Oxford 22.037
	Ländler	Caruthers	BMC
	Mineut in C	Forbes	Schott 10593
	Minuet and Trio	Radmall	Chester 1583a
Müller, J. Frederick	Andante Cantabile		Kjos S5126
	At the Ballet		Kjos S5119
	At the Masquerade		Kjos S5130
	Gavotte Parisienne		Kjos S5124
	Lake Champlain Waltz		Kjos S5129
	Maid of Honor		Kjos S5128
	On the Beach		Kjos S5122
	La Petite Soubrette		Kjos S5125
	Sleigh Ride Party		Kjos S5120
	Summertime		Kjos S5121
	Valse Caprice		Kjos S5127
	Viola Caprice		Kjos S5131
Murray, Eleanor, and Tate, Phyllis	New Viola Books 3 vol.		Oxford 22.813-22.815
Murrill, Herbert (1909-1952)	4 French Nursery Songs		Chester
Novacek, Ottokar (1866-1900)	Mouvement perpétuel (originally for violin)	Ginot	Jobert
Nussio, Otmar (1902-)	Notturno di Valdemosa		UE 12459
Ortiz	Doulce Memoire	Berger	MCA
Paganini, Niccolò (1782-1840)	La Campanella (originally for violin)	Primrose	Schott 10414
	Caprices, op. 1, nos. 13 and 20 (originally for violin)	Forbes-Richardson	Hinrichsen (Pet No. H1984A)
	Caprice no. 9 (originally for violin)	Schimmin	Oxford 22.011
	Caprice no. 24 (originally for violin)	Primrose	CF B2681
	Moto Perpetuo (originally for violin)	Forbes	Oxford 22.036
Paradies, Pietro (1710-1792)	Toccata	Forbes	Oxford 22.107
Paradis, Maria (1759-1824)	Siciliana	Bezrukov	MZK (MCA No. 2314)
Partos, Ödön (1907-)	Oriental Ballade		IMP
Pascal, Andre	Chant sans paroles		Durand
Pasfield, William (1909-)	Barcarolle		Williams 04689
	Chansonette		Williams 04273
	In Playful Mood		Williams 03055

VIOLA AND PIANO (Cont'd)

Composer	Title	Editor	Publisher
Pearson, William	Two Carols		Hinrichsen (Pet No. H319A)
Pepusch, John Christopher (1667-1752)	Largo and Allegro in D Minor		BVP (Pet No. B017)
Pergolesi, Giovanni Battista (1710-1736)	Se tu m'ami	Elkan	Elkan
Persichetti, Vincent (1915-)	Infanta Marina		EV
Peterkin, Norman (1886-)	Twilight Tune		Oxford 20.105
Pisk, Paul (1893-)	3 Movements, op. 36		CFE
Piston, Walter (1894-)	Interlude		BH
Planel, Robert (1908-)	Fantaisie		Leduc
Ponce, Manuel (1882-1948)	Estrellita	Simon-Isaac-Lewis	CF B2378
Popper, David (1843-1913)	Romance		Augener 7637
Porpora, Nicola (1686-1768)	Aria	Tertis	Chester
Porter, Quincy (1897-1966)	Poem Speed Etude		Valley Valley
Pratella	Romanza, op. 24	Pasi	Bongiovanni 796
Prokofiev, Sergey (1891-1953)	Kije's Wedding from Lt. Kije Suite Romance from Lt. Kije Suite Theme and Processional from Peter and the Wolf Selected Pieces from "Romeo and Juliet"	Grunes Borisovsky	EdM EdM Omega MZK (MCA No. 2315)
Pugnani, Gaetano (1731-1798)	Prelude et Allegro	Jurgensen	Jobert
Purcell, Henry (c1659-1695)	Air, Dance, Ground from Dido and Aeneas Airs and Dances Aria Bourrée and Hornpipe Scotch Tune, with Dance	Lutyens Vieland Katims Forbes Forbes	Mills International International Chester Chester
Rachmaninoff, Sergey (1873-1943)	Melodia, op. 3, no. 3 Prelude, op. 23, no. 4 Serenata, op. 3, no. 5	D'Ambrosio D'Ambrosio	Ricordi 119233 MZK (MCA No. 2311) Ricordi 119234
Raff, Joachim (1822-1882)	Cavatina (originally for violin)	Ritter-Schloming	CF B1292
Rafter, Leonard (1911-)	5 Pieces		Bosworth
Rakov	Tale		MZK (MCA No. 2317)
Rameau, Jean-Philippe (1683-1764)	Rigaudon Suite of 3 Dances	Applebaum Forbes-Richardson	Belwin Oxford 22.014

Composer	Title	Editor	Publisher
Rapoport	Poem		Mercury
Ravel, Maurice (1875-1937)	Pavane pour une Infante défunte (originally for piano)	Kochanski	Eschig 1463D
	Pavane pour une Infante défunte	Maganini	EdM
	Pièce en forme de Habanera (originally for voice)		Leduc
Rebikow, Vladimir (1866-1920)	Berceuse and Dance	Forbes	Chester
Reger, Max (1873-1916)	Romance in G	Sitt	BRH
Reinhold, Otto (1899-)	Musik		Bärenreiter 1988
Reizenstein, Franz (1911-)	Concert Fantasy, op. 42		Heinrichsen (Pet No. H509)
Rendall, Honor	Island Lullaby		Williams W1417
	Island Reel		Williams W1418
Renosto	Avent d'ecrire		Ricordi 130999
Reutter, Hermann (1900-)	Musik		Schott
Richardson, Alan (1904-)	Autumn Sketches		Oxford 22.101
Richter, Marga (1926-)	Aria and Toccata		Mills
Rimsky-Korsakov, Nickolay (1844-1908)	Dance of the Buffons	Strakhov	MZK (MCA No. 2321)
	Song of India	Deery	CF B2350
Rolland and Fletcher	First Perpetual Motion		Mills
Ropartz, J. Guy (1864-1955)	Adagio		RL
Rötscher, Konrad (1910-)	Musik, op. 27		BB
Rougnon, Paul	Fantaisie-Caprice		Leduc
Rowley, Alex (1892-1958)	Aubade		Williams (Mil No. W1403-1)
	Farandole		Williams (Mil No. W1403-4)
	Reverie		Williams (Mil No. W1403-3)
	Scherzo		Williams (Mil No. W1403-2
Rubinstein, Anton (1829-1894)	Three Morceaux		Hamelle
	Romance	Cheyette	Fox
Russell, Henry (1812-1900)	Life on the Ocean Wave		Kjos S-5105
Russotto, Leo (1896-1943)	Arioso		MPH
	Novelette		MPH
	Poeme		MPH
Saint-Saëns, Camille (1835-1921)	Le Cygne, from Le Carnaval des Animaux	Gottlieb	CF B1393
	Melody	Tertis	GS

VIOLA AND PIANO (Cont'd)

Composer	Title	Editor	Publisher
Sárai, Tibor (1919-)	Humoresque		Kultura
Schäfer, Gerhart (1926-)	Espressioni 4 Kleine Stücke		Simrock Gerig 345
Scheer, Leo	Lament		CP
Schlemüller, Hugo	Our Soldiers, op. 12, no. 5 Prayer, op. 12, no. 6 Song, op. 12, no. 1		CF B2323 CF B2324 CF B2322
Schmitt, Florent (1870-1958)	Légende, op. 66		Durand
Schmitt, Jacob	Spring Song	Applebaum	Belwin
Schollum, Robert (1913-)	Chaconne, op. 54a		Doblinger
Schubert, Franz (1797-1828)	Ave Marie The Bee Litany for All Saints Day 3 Minuets Reverie	Primrose Ginot Primrose Piatigorsky Elkan Forbes	Schott Jobert Schott 5577 EV Oxford
Schumann, Robert (1810-1856)	Adagio and Allegro, op. 70 Adagio and Allegro, op. 70 Märchenbilder, op. 113 Märchenbilder, "Pictures from Fairyland" Märchenbilder, "Fairy Tales" Romance in F, op. 28, no. 2 (originally for piano) Romance in F Romance and Merry Peasant 3 Romances, op. 94 (originally for oboe) Träumerei, op. 15, no. 7 4 Pieces, op. 113	Vieland Schradieck Tertis Jacobson Kreuz Strakhov	International Peters 2386 BRH GS L415 Peters 2372 Augener Cramer Augener Augener 7641 CF B2363 MZK (MCA No. 2322)
Schwartz, Maximilian (1899-)	Theme and Variations		BRH
Scriabin, Alexander (1872-1915)	Etude, op. 2, no. 1 (originally for piano) Prelude, op. 9 Prelude, op. 9, no. 1	Krane Borisovsky Krane	GS 43049 International Spratt
Seiber, Mátyás (1905-1960)	Elegie	Banks	Schott 10422
Seitz, Albert	Fantaisie de concert, op. 31		Leduc
Senaillé, Jean Baptiste (1687-1730)	Allegro Spiritoso	Katims	International
Seter, Mordecai (1916-)	Elegy		IMI
Shapey, Ralph (1921-)	Duo		CFE
Shield, William (1748-1829)	Tempo di Menuetto	Anderson	Oxford

Composer	Title	Editor	Publisher
Shore, Bernard (1896-)	Scherzo		Augener
Shostakovitch, Dmitri (1906-)	3 Pieces: Overture, Romance, Contradance 3 Pieces: Barrel-Organ Waltz, Nocturne, Galop	Borisovsky Borisovsky	MZK (MCA No. 2324) MZK (MCA No. 2325)
Shulman, Alan (1915-)	Homage to Erik Satie		GS
Siennicki	Woodland Waltz		Kjos S5123
Simon	Lullaby for Johnny		EdM
Simonetti, Achille (1857-1928)	Allegretto romantico Ballata		Chester Chester
Sitt, Hans (1850-1922)	Album Leaves, op. 39 Album Leaves		International Peters 2549
Smith, Julia (1911-)	2 Pieces	Doktor	Mowbray
Somervell, Arthur (1863-1937)	School of Melody	Mackinlay	Augener
Spendiarov, Alexander (1871-1928)	Lullaby		MZK
Spies, Leo (1899-)	5 Sommerbilder Viopiacem		BRH BH
Steiner, Georg (1900-)	Rhapsodic Poem		MZK
Stepanov, Lev (1908-)	Miniatures, from Children's Suite		MZK (MCA No. 2327)
Stepanova, V.	Poem		MZK (MCA No. 2329)
Stevens, Halsey (1908-)	3 Hungarian Folk Songs 3 Hungarian Folk Songs		CFE Highgate
Stewart, Robert	3 Short Pieces		CFE
Strauss, Richard (1864-1949)	Don Quixote, op. 35	Johnson	Chester 7093
Stravinski, Igor (1882-)	Berceuse Dance of the Princesses		EdM EdM
Stojowski, Zygmunt (1869-1946)	Fantasia	Szaleski	PWM
Swain, Freda (1902-)	English Reel Song at Evening		Williams 04870 Williams 03552
Szabó, Ferenc (1902-)	Air		Kultura
Szekely, Endre (1912-)	Rhapsody no. 1		Kultura
Tal, Joseph (1910-)	Duo		IMI
Taneyev, Alexander (1850-1918)	Album Leaves, op. 33		MZK (MCA No. 2331)
Tartini, Giuseppi (1692-1770)	Adagio and Fugue Sarabande	Radmall	Chester MZK
Tausinger, Jan (1921-)	Partita		Panton

VIOLA AND PIANO (Cont'd)

Composer	Title	Editor	Publisher
Tchaikovsky, Peter Ilyich (1840-1893)	Autumn Song, op. 37	Borisovsky	MZK (MCA No. 2332)
	Aveux Passione	Borisovsky	MZK (MCA No. 2333)
	By the Fireside, op. 31, no. 1		MZK (MCA No. 2334)
	Chanson Triste, op. 40, no. 2	Isaac-Lewis	CF B2364
	Lullaby, from Mazeppa	Strakhov	MZK (MCA No. 2335)
	Melody, op. 42, no. 3	Strakhov	MZK (MCA No. 2536)
	Nocturne, op. 19, no. 4	Borisovsky	International
	Nocturne; Snowdrop	Borisovsky	MZK (MCA No. 2337)
	None But the Lonely Heart, op. 6, no. 6	Hegner-Deery	CF B2352
	None But the Lonely Heart		Mills
	Passionate Confession		MZK
	Serenade		Paxton
	Snowdrop, op. 37, no. 4	Borisovsky	MZK (MCA No. 2338)
	Song Without Words, op. 2, no. 3	Strakhov	MZK (MCA No. 2339)
	Sweet Day-dream		MZK (MCA No. 2341)
	Theme from Symphony no. 5	Caruthers	BMC
	Valse Sentimentale, op. 51, no. 6	Grunes	Omega
	Valse Sentimentale		MZK
	Variations on a Rococo Theme, op. 33	Robin-Primrose	Western
	White Knights, op. 37, no. 5	Borisovsky	MZK (MCA No. 2340)
Tertis, Lionel (1876-)	Blackbirds		Augener
	Sunset		Chester
	Tune		Augener
Thomas, Ambroise (1811-1896)	Gavotte from Mignon	Isaac-Lewis	CF B2380
Ticciati, Niso (1924-)	Minuet and Berceuse	Copperwheat	Oxford 22.040
	Scherzo and Toccata	Copperwheat	Oxford 22.041
Tiessen, Heinz (1887-)	Tinker's Dance	Sontag	SB
	2 Serious Melodies		RE (Pet. No. RE12)
Trantow, Herbert (1903-)	Duo (1936)		MV (Pet No. MV1023)
Trimble	Duo		Peters 66076
Tsintsadze, Sulkhan (1925-)	Khorumi		MZK
Turina, Joaquin (1882-1949)	Andante, from Sevilla		MZK
Tzitovich	Triptych		MZK (MCA No. 2342)
Vale	Ao pé da fogueira	Heifetz-Primrose	CF B2673
Valensin, Georges	Minuet	Katims	International
Vaughan Williams, Ralph (1872-1958)	Fantasia on Greensleeves	Forbes	Oxford 22.001
	Romance		Oxford
	6 Studies in English Folk Song		STB
Veprik, Alexander (1899-1958)	Rhapsody, op. 11		MZK (MCA No. 2340)
Veracini, Francesco (1690-c1750)	Largo	Katims	International

Composer	Title	Editor	Publisher
Verstovsky, Alexey (1799-1862)	Variations on Two Themes	Borisovsky	MZK (MCA No. 2344)
Vieux, Maurice (1884-)	Étude de Concert No. 1 in C		Eschig
	Étude de Concert No. 2 in B Minor		Eschig
	Étude de Concert No. 3 in G		Eschig
	Étude de Concert No. 4 in F Minor		Eschig
	Étude de Concert No. 5 in C sharp Minor		Eschig
	Étude de Concert No. 6 in F sharp Minor		Eschig
	Scherzo		Leduc
Vieuxtemps, Henri (1820-1881)	Elégie, op. 30	Scholz	Augener 7648
	Elégie, op. 30		Sikorski 305
Villa Lobos, Heitor (1887-1959)	Aria from Bachianas Brasileiras no. 5	Primrose	AMP
Vitali, Tommaso Antonio (c1644-1692)	Ciaccona (originally for violin)	Bailly	GS
	Ciaccona	Petri	BRH
Vivaldi, Antonio (1669-1741	Adagio and Allegro	Jacob	Novello
	Intermezzo from Concerto Grosso in D Minor	Franko	GS
Vlag, Harrand (1913-)	Ballade		Heuwek
Vreuls, Victor (1876-1944)	Poeme		Bosworth
Wagner, Richard (1813-1883)	Entrance of the Black Swans	Polo	SZ
	Song of the Evening Star	Isaac-Lewis	CF B2381
	Traüme	Primrose	Schott 10413
Walker, Ernest (1870-1949)	Romance, op. 9		Williams (Mil No. W1422)
	Variations on an original theme		Novello
Walthew, Richard (1872-1951)	Regret and Conversation Galante		BH 5635
Ward, Robert (1917-)	Arioso		Highgate
	Tarantelle		Highgate
Warren, Elinor (1905-)	Poem		CF B2741
Weber, Carl Maria von (1786-1826)	Andante u Rondo ungarese, op. 35	Schunemann	Schott 2645
	Andante u Rondo ungarese	Primrose	International
	Serenata, op. 3, no. 1	Forbes	Schott 10653
--	When Love Is Kind	Buchtel	Kjos S5102
Whittenberg, Charles	Set for 2		CFE
Wieniawski, Henri (1835-1880)	Alla Saltarella, op. 10, no. 4	Forbes	Hinrichsen
	Alla Tarantella, op. 18, no. 4		(Pet No. H3368A)
Wigglesworth, Frank (1918-)	Sound Piece		CFE
Winkler, Alexander (1865-1935)	Meditation Elegiaque, op. 31, no. 1		BH 3397
	La Toupie, op. 31, no. 2		BH 2298
Wolstenholme, William (1865-1931)	Allegretto		Novello
	Canzona	Tertis	Novello
	Romanza		Novello

VIOLA AND PIANO (Cont'd)

Composer	Title	Editor	Publisher
Wood, Hugh (1932-)	Variations		UE 12911
Work, Henry (1832-1884)	Grandfather's Clock		Belwin
Zafred, Mario (1922-)	Elegia in 3 tempi		Ricordi 130818
Zich, Otakar (1879-1934)	Elegie		Artia

TEACHING PIECES SERIES Published separately

First Series: 1st position

Composer	Title		Publisher
Bach, Johann Sebastian (1685-1750)	Gavotte, from French Suite no. 6		Augener
Beethoven, Ludwig van (1770-1827)	Sonatina and Romanze		Augener
Fitzenhagen, W.	Cavatina		Augener
Gluck, Christoph (1714-1787)	Air		Augener
Haydn, Joseph (1732-1809)	Air		Augener
Kreuz, Emil (1867-1932)	Gavotte		Augener
	Melody		Augener
	Pensée fugitive		Augener
	Romance		Augener
Mendelssohn, Felix (1809-1847)	Venetian Gondola Song		Augener
Schubert, Franz (1797-1828)	Fishermaiden		Augener
Schumann, Robert (1810-1856)	Canon and Reaper's Song		Augener
	Humming Song and Hunting Song		Augener
	Melody and Soldiers' March		Augener
	Romance and Merry Peasant		Augener
	Siciliano		Augener
Weber, Carl Maria von (1786-1926)	Air		Augener

Second Series: 1st to 3rd position

Composer	Title		Publisher
Gluck, Christoph (1714-1787)	Ballet, from Orfeo		Augener
Gurlitt, Cornelius (1820-1901)	Buds and Blossoms		Augener
	Slow Waltz		Augener
Handel, Georg Friedrich (1685-1759)	Largo		Augener
	Sonata		Augener
Kjerulf, Halfdan (1815-1868)	Longing		Augener

Composer	Title	Editor	Publisher
Mendelssohn, Felix (1809-1847)	Song Without Words, op. 38, no. 2 Song Without Words, op. 53, no. 4		Augener Augener
Schubert, Franz (1797-1828)	Serenade		Augener
Schumann, Robert (1810-1856)	Revery		Augener
Weber, Carl Maria von (1786-1826)	Air		Augener

Third Series: 1st-7th position

Composer	Title	Editor	Publisher
Bach, Johann Sebastian (1685-1750)	Air, from Orchestral Suite in D		Augener
Beethoven, Ludwig van (1770-1827)	Romance in F, op. 50		Augener
Goltermann, G.	Romance		Augener
Kreuz, Emil (1867-1932)	Liebesbilder Spring Fancies		Augener Augener
Mendelssohn, Felix (1809-1847)	Song Without Words, op. 19, no. 1		Augener
Meyerbeer, Giacomo (1791-1864)	Air		Augener
Schubert, Franz (1797-1828)	Romance		Augener
Schumann, Robert (1810-1856)	Evening Song Little Study Stück im Volkston		Augener Augener Augener
Squire, William (1871-1963)	Gavotte humoristiques Reverie		Augener Augener

COLLECTIONS OF SOLOS

Editor	Title	Publisher
Applebaum	Building Technique with Beautiful Music 4 vol.	Belwin
Bagrintzer, A.	Viola Solos from Ballets	MZK (MCA No. 2284)
Berger	Viola Solos for Study and Performance	MCA
Boetze	Viola Music for Concert and Church	BMC
Bornoff	Fiddler's Holiday	CF 04248
Brodszky	Old Music (XVII and XVIII Centuries) Old Music	Kultura EdM
Conus, Katims and Borisovsky	Album of 6 Pieces	International
Dodd	Viola Album	Schott 10900
Doktor	Solos for the Viola Player	GS 44399
Eckard	Highlights of Familiar Music	Presser
Forbes	Classical Pieces 2 vol.	Oxford 22.013, 22.035
Forbes	First Year Classical Album	Oxford 22.809
Forbes	Second Year Classical Album	Oxford 22.038

COLLECTIONS OF SOLOS (Cont'd)

Editor	Title	Publisher
Gifford	12 Irish Airs	Schott
Harvey	Viola Players Repertory	Presser
Herfurth	Classical Album	BMC 12637
Herfurth-Devertitch	Viola and Piano	Willis
——	Highlights of Familiar Music	Presser
Hudaloff	24 Selected Compositions	Pro Art
Isaac	Melody Book for Strings	CF 03828
Klengel	Album of 24 Classical Pieces 3 vol.	International
Klengel	Classic Pieces 3 vol.	Peters 3853 AbC
Klengel	Viola Album of Classical Pieces	Peters 7074
Kreuz	The Violist, op. 13 3 vol.	Augener 763a,b,c
Lovell	44 Easy Tunes	Oxford 22.810
Meyer	Alte Meister des Violaspiels	Peters 3816
	Hammer: 3 Sonatas, Sonata for viola d'amore	
	Stamitz: Concerto in D	
Moffatt and Laubach	Classical Album	Augener 5566
Murray and Tate	Tunes Old and New	Oxford 22.811
Palaschko	Alte Meister für junge Spieler	Schott 1338
Reitikh	5 Pieces by Russian and Soviet Composers	MZK 2385
Reitikh, M.	Anthology of Teaching Repertoire, 2 vol.	MZK (MCA No. 2318)
Rood	Old Dances for Young Violas	MM
Simon	Classical Solo Compositions	EdM
Simon	Concert Album	EdM
Stehling	Album of Celebrated Pieces	Augener 7625a
Strakhov	Pieces by Russian and Soviet Composers 2 vol.	MZK
Szaleski	Works by Polish Composers for Viola	PWM
——	Viola Miniatures	CF 04260
——	34 Viola Solos	Belwin EL236
Whistler	Solos for Strings	Rubank 797
Whistler and Hummel	Concert and Contest Album	Rubank
Widdicombe	First Book of Viola Pieces	Chester

III LARGE WORKS

CONCERTOS, CONCERTINOS, COMPOSITIONS WITH ORCHESTRA

Composer	Title	Editor	Publisher
Accolay, J. B. (1845-1910)	Concerto No. 1 (originally for violin and piano)	Doty	GS L1785
Angerer, Paul (1927-)	Concerto, 1962		Doblinger
Antufeyev, B.	Concerto, op. 45		MZK (MCA No. 7282)

Composer	Title	Editor	Publisher
Aristakesian, E.	Concerto		MZK (MCA No. 2283)
Bach, Johann Christian (1735-1782)	Concerto in C Minor	Casadesus	Salabert 5457
Bach, Johann Christoph (1642-1703)	Concerto in E flat	Sieler-Kübart-Roetscher	BB
Bach, Johann Sebastian (1685-1750)	Brandenburg Concerto no. 6 for two violas		Hinrichsen (Pet No. H670)
Bach, Karl Philipp Emanuel (1714-1788)	Concerto in A Minor (originally for violoncello and orchestra)		Leduc
	Concerto in B flat (originally for violoncello and orchestra)	Klengel	BRH
	Concerto	Casadesus	GS
Baeyens, August (1895-)	Concerto		Metropolis
Bancquart, Alain (1934-)	Concerto		Jobert
Bartel, Hans-Christian (1932-)	Concerto		DVM
Bartók, Béla (1881-1945)	Concerto	Serly	BH 16854
Bax, Arnold (1883-1953)	Phantasy		Chappell
Beck, Conrad (1901-)	Concerto		Schott 4329
Becker, John (1886-1961)	Concerto		CFE
Benda, Georg (1722-1795)	Konzert in F	Lebermann	Schott 5682
Benjamin, Arthur (1893-1960)	Concerto or Sonata		BH
	Romantic Fantasy (for violin, viola, and orchestra)		BH
Berlioz, Hector (1803-1968)	Harold in Italy	Liszt-Riley	UMP
Blacher, Boris (1903-)	Concerto, op. 48		BB
Bloch, Ernest (1880-1959)	Concertino (for flute, viola, and orchestra)		GS
	Suite		GS
	Suite Hebraique		GS
Boccherini, Luigi (1743-1805)	Concerto no. 3 in G (originally for violoncello and orchestra)	Ross	GS L1726
Borup-Jørgensen, Axel (1924-)	Music for Percussion and Viola, op. 18		DM
Bozza, Eugène (1905-)	Concertino		Ricard
Braein, Edvard (1887-1957)	Serenade		Lyche

CONCERTOS, CONCERTINOS, COMPOSITIONS WITH ORCHESTRA (Cont'd)

Composer	Title	Editor	Publisher
Brixi, Franz (1732-1771)	Konzert in C	Lebermann	Schott 5961
Bruch, Max (1838-1920)	Romanze, op. 85		Schott 1974
Bunin, Revol (1924-)	Concerto, op. 22	Barshai	MZK (MCA No. 2288)
Burkhard, Willy (1900-1955)	Konzert		Bärenreiter 2786
Chevreville, Raymond (1901-)	Double Concerto, op. 34, for viola, piano, and orchestra		BCM
Clarke, Henry (1907-)	Encounters		CFE
Collet, Henri (1885-1951)	Rhapsodie Castillane		Senart
Cooley, Carlton	Concertino		Elkan
Cowell, Henry (1897-1965)	Variations on Thirds for 2 violas and orchestra		Peters
David, Gyula (1913-)	Concerto		Kultura
David	Concertino		Billaudot
De Jong, Marinus (1891-)	Concerto, op. 111		BCM
Diercks, John (1927-)	Diversion from violin, viola, and orchestra		Tritone
Dittersdorf, Karl Ditters von (1739-1799)	Konzert in F	Lebermann	Schott 5054
	Cadenza for Konzert in F (Hanesyan)		Eschig
	Symphonie Concertante in D for viola, double-bass, and orchestra		International
	Symphonie Concertante in D for viola, double-bass, and orchestra		Hofmeister
Druschetzky, Georg	Concerto in D	Schwamberger	Simrock
Dunhill, Thomas (1877-1946)	Triptych		Oxford
Dvořák, Antonin (1841-1904)	Concerto, op. 104 (originally for violoncello and orchestra)	Vieland	International
Elgar, Edward (1857-1934)	Concerto (originally for violoncello and orchestra)	Tertis	Novello
Enesco, Georges (1881-1955)	Concertpiece		International 642
Forsyth, Cecil (1870-1941)	Konzert in G Minor	Ireland	Schott 1077
Fricker, Racine (1920-)	Concerto, op. 20		Schott 10270
Ghedini, Giorgio (1892-1965)	Musica da Concerto for viola or viola d'amore		Ricordi

Composer	Title	Editor	Publisher
Giuffré, Gaetano (1918-)	Concerto		Ricordi 130727
Glanville-Hicks, Peggy (1912-)	Concerto Romantico		CFE
Goeb, Roger (1914-)	Concertante no. 3 in C		CFE
Golestan, Stan (1862-1956)	Arioso et Allegro de Concert		Salabert
Golubev, Evgeny (1910-)	Concerto, op. 47		MZK (MCA No. 2299)
Gorner, Hans-Georg	Concertino, op. 31 for violin, viola, and piano		Hofmeister
Graun, Johann (1703-1771)	Concerto in C Minor for violin, viola, and orchestra		BRH
Green, Ray (1909-)	Concertante		Amphion
Handel, Georg Friedrich (1685-1759)	Concerto in B Minor	Casadesus	Eschig 1311
	Concerto in B Minor		AMP
	Cadenza for Concerto in B Minor (Hanesyan)		Eschig
	Concerto	Barbirolli	Oxford 22.012
Handoshkin, Ivan (1747-1804) (see Khandoshkin)	Concerto		International 2067
Hartmann, Karl (1905-1963)	Konzert for viola, piano, and orchestra		Schott 4624
Haug, Hans (1900-)	Fantasia Concertante		Curci
Haydn, Joseph (1732-1809)	Concerto in D (originally for violoncello and orchestra)	Gevaert	BRH
	Concerto in D	Spitzner	International
	Concerto (originally for oboe and orchestra		MZK
Hankemans, Hans (1913-)	Concerto		Donemus
Hindemith, Paul (1895-1963	Kammermusik no. 5, Concerto op. 36, no. 4		Schott 1977
	Konzertmusik, op. 48		Schott 3150
	Trauermusik, 1936		Schott 2515
	Trauermusik, 1936		AMP
	Der Schwanendreher		Schott 2517
Hoddinott, Alun (1929-)	Concertino		Oxford 22.409
Hoffmeister, Franz (1754-1812)	Concerto in D		Grahl (Pet No. GR 9)
	Concerto in D	Doktor	International
	Concerto in D	Ferraguzzi	Curci
	Cadenza for Concerto in D (Hanesyan)		Eschig
	Concerto	Vieux	Eschig
Hofstetter, Roman (1742-1815)	Konzert in C	Lebermann	Schott 5962
	Concerto in E flat		WM (Pet No. WM 111)
Holst, Gustav (1874-1934)	Lyric Movement		Oxford 77.412
Honnoré, Leon	Morceau de Concert	Wael-Munk	Gilles

CONCERTOS, CONCERTINOS, COMPOSITIONS WITH ORCHESTRA (Cont'd)

Composer	Title	Editor	Publisher
Hovhaness, Alan (1911-)	Talin Concerto, op. 93		AMP 95927
Howels, Herbert (1892-)	Elegy for viola, string quartet, and orchestra		BH
Hüe, Georges (1858-1948)	Theme Varié		Heugel
Huggler, John	Divertimento, op. 32		Peters 6863
Husa, Karel (1921-)	Poem		Schott
Jacob, Gordon (1895-)	Concerto		Oxford
Jongen, Joseph (1873-1953)	Suite		Lemoine
Josephs, Wilfred (1927-)	Meditatio de Beornmundo, op. 30		Hinrichsen
Kalaš, Julius (1902-)	Concerto in D Minor, op. 69		Panton
Kelemen, Milko (1924-)	3 Dances		UE
Khandoshkin, Ivan (1747-1804) (see Handoshkin)	Concerto		MZK (MCA No. 2303)
Koetsier, Jan (1911-)	Concerto		Sirius
Kohs, Ellis (1916-)	Chamber Concerto		Mercury
Koppel, Herman (1908-)	Concerto, op. 43 for violin, viola and orchestra		Hansen
Kreutzer, Rodolphe (1766-1831)	Concerto no. 9 (originally for violin and orchestra)	Ginot	Jobert
	Concerto no. 13 (originally for violin and orchestra)	Ginot	Jobert
Kreuz, Emil (1867-1932)	Concerto in C, op. 20		Augener 5571
Krol, Bernhard (1920-)	Konzertante Musik, op. 6		BRH
Kubik, Gail (1914-)	Symphony Concertante for trumpet, viola, piano, and orchestra		FC
Kurtag, György (1926-)	Concerto		Kultura
Lalo, Edouard (1832-1892)	Concerto in D Minor (originally for violoncello and orchestra)	Casadesus	International
Larsson, Lars-Erik (1908-)	Concertino, op. 45, no. 9		Gehrmans
Ledenyov, R.	Concerto-Poem, op. 13		MZK (MCA No. 2312)
Lo Presti, Ronald	Nocturne		CF

Composer	Title	Editor	Publisher
Lutyens, Elizabeth (1906-)	Concerto, op. 15		Lengnick (Mil No. L2000)
Maconchy, Elizabeth	Concerto		Lengnick
Maes, Jef (1905-)	Concerto		BCM
Malige, Fred (1895-)	Concerto		BRH
Malipiero, Gian (1882-)	Dialoghi V		Ricordi
Martinu, Bohuslav (1890-1959)	Rhapsody Concerto		Bärenreiter
Mendelssohn, Ludwig	Student Concerto	Klotman	CF C152
Meulemans, Arthur (1884-)	Concerto		BCM
Milford, Robin (1903-1959)	Elegiac Meditation		Oxford 22.030
Milhaud, Darius (1892-)	Concertino d'Eté		Heugel
	Concerto		UE 3718
	Concerto No. 2		Heugel
Mortari, Virgilio (1902-)	Concerto dell 'oservanza, 1965		Ricordi 131243
Mozart, Wolfgang Amadeus (1756-1791)	Concerto in A, K622 (originally for clarinet and orchestra)	Tertis	International Chester
	Concerto in A, K622 (originally for clarinet and orchestra)	Strakhov	MZK (MCA No. 2312)
	Concerto K216 (originally for violin and orchestra)	Fuchs	MPH
	Concerto No. 3 (originally for horn and orchestra)	Strakhov	MZK (MCA No. 2313)
	Sinfonia Concertante in E flat, K364 for violin, viola, and orchestra		Augener, BRH Broude, GS, GT Kalmus
Müller-Zürich, Paul (1898-)	Concerto, op. 24		Schott 3289
Nussio, Otmar (1902-)	Notturno di Valdemosa		UE 12459
Paganini, Niccolò (1782-1840)	Terzetto Concertante in D for viola, violoncello, and guitar		ZM
Pannain, Guido (1891-)	Concerto		Curci
Parris, Robert (1924-)	Concerto		CFE
Partos, Ödön (1907-)	Concerto no. 1		IMP
	Concerto no. 2		IMP
	Sinfonia Concertante, Concerto no. 3		IMI
	Yiskor		MCA
Perle, George	Serenade for viola and solo instruments		Presser
Pinelli, Carlo	Concerto		Ricordi
Piston, Walter (1894-)	Concerto		AMP

CONCERTOS, CONCERTINOS, COMPOSITIONS WITH ORCHESTRA (Cont'd)

Composer	Title	Editor	Publisher
Pleyel, Ignaz (1757-1831)	Concerto in D, op. 31		Grahl (Pet No. GR 10)
Porter, Quincy (1897-1966)	Concerto		AMP
Quinet, Marcel	Concerto		BCM
Read, Gardner (1913-)	Fantasy, op. 38		AMP
	Poem, op. 31a		CF B2675
Reed, William (1876-1942)	Rhapsody in D		Augener
Rivier, Jean (1896-)	Concertino		Salabert 8843
Rode, Pierre (1774-1830)	Concerto no. 7 (originally for violin and orchestra)	Ginot	Jobert
	Concerto no. 8 (originally for violin and orchestra)	Ginot	Jobert
Rohwer, Jens (1914-)	Chamber Concerto for violin, viola, and string orchestra		Möseler
Rolla, Alessandro (1757-1841)	Concerto in E flat, op. 3	Beck	FC 1541
Rosenberg, Hilding (1892-)	Concerto		Nordiska
Rougnon, Paul	Concerto romantique		Hamelle
Rubbra, Edmund (1901-)	Concerto in A		Lengnick (Mil No. L2009)
Schäfer, Karl (1899-)	Divertimento über Thema von Conrad Paumann		Gerig 362
Schubert, Joseph (1757-1833)	Konzert in C	Schultz-Hauser	Schott 5322
Seitz, Friedrich (1848-1918)	Concerto no. 2, op. 13 (originally for violin and orchestra)	Lifschey	AMP
	Concerto no. 3, op. 12 (originally for violin and orchestra)	Lifschey	AMP
	Concerto no. 4 (originally for violin and orchestra)	Caruthers	BMC
	Concerto no. 5 in D, op. 22 (originally for violin and orchestra)	Klotman	Mills
Serly, Tibor (1900-)	Concerto		MCA
	Rhapsody		SMP
Seter, Mordecai (1916-)	Elegy		IMI
Shulman, Alan (1915-)	Theme and Variations		Chappell
Sitt, Hans (1850-1922)	Concert Piece in G, op. 46		Eulenberg (Pet No. ES129)
	Concert Piece in G, op. 46		International 1196
	Concert Piece in G, op. 46		Lengnick

Composer	Title	Editor	Publisher
Sobanski, Hans (1906-)	Romantic Concerto		UE 11135
Stamitz, Anton (1754-1809)	Konzert No. 2 in F	Lebermann	Schott 5956
Stamitz, Johann (1717-1757)	Concerto in G	Laugg	Peters 5889
Stamitz, Karl (1745-1801)	Concerto in D, op. 1	Klengel	BRH
	Concerto in D, op. 1	Meyer	International 542
	Concerto in D, op. 1		Peters 3816A
	Concerto in D, op. 1	Polo	Ricordi ER1762
	Cadenza for Concerto in D (Hanesyan)		Eschig
	Sinfonia Concertante in D for violin, viola, and orchestra		Kneusslin
Starer, Robert (1924-)	Concerto		MCA
Steiner, Hugo	Concerto in D Minor, op. 43		International 1524
Stout, Alan (1932-)	Velut Umbra, op. 35 for flute, viola, and orchestra		CFE
Stratton, George (1897-1954)	Pastorale Concerto		Novello
Tansman, Alexander (1897-)	Concerto		Eschig
Tartini, Giuseppe (1692-1770)	Concerto in D (originally for violin and orchestra)	Vieux	Eschig
Tchaikowsky, Peter (1840-1893)	Variations on a Theme Rococo, op. 33 (originally for violoncello and orchestra)	Robin-Primrose	Western
Telemann, Georg Philipp (1681-1767)	Concerto in G	Courte	Elkan
	Concerto in G	Füssl	Bärenreiter 3712
	Concerto in G	Katims	International
	Concerto in G	Szaleski	PWM
	Cadenza for Concerto in G (Hanesyan)		Eschig
Tlil, Amali	Concerto		Jobert
Tomasi, Henri (1901-)	Concerto		Leduc
Tselter	Concerto		MZK
Vaňhal, Jan (1739-1813)	Concerto in C	Blažek-Plichta	Artia
Vardi, Emanuel (1915-)	Suite on American Folk Songs		GS
Vaughan Williams, Ralph (1872-1958)	Suite 3 vol.		Oxford 22.008-22.010
Veress, Sándor (1907-)	Ungarischer Werbetanz		UE
Vieuztemps, Henri (1820-1881)	Concerto no. 2 (originally for violin and orchestra)	Ginot	Jobert
	Concerto no. 4 (originally for violin and orchestra)	Ginot	Jobert
	Concerto no. 5 (originally for violin and orchestra)	Ginot	Jobert

CONCERTOS, CONCERTINOS, COMPOSITIONS WITH ORCHESTRA (Cont'd)

Composer	Title	Editor	Publisher
Viotti, Giovanni (1755-1824)	Concerto no. 22 (originally for violin and orchestra)	Ginot	Jobert
	Concerto no. 29 (originally for violin and orchestra)	Ginot	Jobert
Vivaldi, Antonio (c1669-1741)	Concerto in A	Townsend	Ricordi 2532
	Concerto no. 19 in A (originally for violin and orchestra)	Oubradous	Transatlantiques
	Concerto in B flat Minor (originally for viola d'amore and orchestra)	Courte	CF
	Concerto in E (originally for viola d'amore and orchestra)	Courte	CF
	Concerto in E Minor	Primrose	International 2067
	Concerto (originally for viola d'amore and orchestra)	Borisovsky	MZK 2409
	Concerto	Primrose	Mills
	Concerto	Nagy	BH
	Sonata in B flat	Primrose	International
Walton, William (1902-)	Concerto		Oxford 22.006
Weber, Ben (1916-)	Rhapsodie Concertante		CFE
Westermann, Helmut (1895-)	Konzertante Musik, op. 34		Simrock
Wieniawski, Henri (1835-1880)	Concerto no. 2 (originally for violin and orchestra)	Ginot	Jobert
Wigglesworth, Frank	Concertino		CFE
Wranitzki, Anton (1761-1820)	Concerto in C for 2 violas and piano		Hofmeister
Zafred, Mario (1922-)	Concerto		Ricordi 129165
Zelter, Karl (1758-1832)	Concerto in E flat		Grahl (Pet No. GR 11)
	Cadenza for Concerto in E flat (Hanesyan)		Eschig
Zimmermann, Bernd (1918-)	Antiphonen		EDW

SONATAS, SONATINAS, SUITES, DIVERTIMENTOS
for viola and piano unless otherwise specified
for solo sonatas see section II Viola Alone

Composer	Title	Editor	Publisher
Ariosti, Attilio (1660-1740)	Sonata		MZK
	2 Sonatas in E Minor and in C		Schott 5958
	2 Sonatas (originally for viola d'amore)	Renzo	Santis 981
Arne, Thomas (1710-1778)	Sonata in B flat	Craxton	Oxford 20.007
Arnold, Malcolm (1921-)	Sonata		Lengnick (Mil No. L2003)
Avshalomov, Jacob (1919-)	Sonatine		Mercury

Composer	Title	Editor	Publisher
Bach, Johann Sebastian (1685-1750)	6 Sonatas 2 vol. (originally for violin and clavier) 2 vol.	David-Hermann	International 866
	3 Sonatas (originally for gamba)	Consolini	Ricordi ER116
	3 Sonatas	Forbes	Peters 4286A
	3 Sonatas	Naumann	BRH, International
	Sonata in F	Forbes	Peters 4460A
	Suite in F	Courte	Elkan
Bach, Karl Philipp Emanuel (1714-1788)	Sonata in G Minor	Primrose	International
	Sonata in G Minor	Ruff	Schott 5953
Bach, Wilhelm Friedemann (1710-1784)	Sonata in C Minor (viola and harpsichord or piano)	Pessl	Oxford 22.801
Badings, Henk (1907-)	Sonata		Donemus (Pet No. D3)
Bantock, Granville (1868-1946)	Sonata in F		Chester
Bassett, Leslie (1923-)	Sonata		CFE
Bauer, Marion (1887-1955)	Sonata		SPAM
Bax, Arnold (1883-1953)	Fantasy-Sonata (for harp and viola)		Chappell
	Sonata		Chappell 38180
Beethoven, Ludwig van (1770-1827)	Notturno	Beck	GS 41948
	Notturno	Primrose	Schott
	Sonata in G Minor, op. 5, no. 2 (originally for violoncello and piano)	Tertis	Augener
	Sonata in G Minor		International
	Sonata, op. 17 (originally for horn and piano)		International
	Sonata in F, op. 24 (originally for violin and piano)	Forbes	Peters 4066b
	Sonata in A, op. 69 (originally for violoncello and piano)		International
	Sonatina and Romance	Kreuz	Augener
Benjamin, Arthur (1893-1960)	Sonata or Concerto		BH
Berkeley, Lennox (1903-)	Sonata in D Minor		Chester
Binder, Christlieb (1723-1789)	Sonata in D	Ruf	Schott 5357
Blackwood, Easley (1933-)	Sonata		EV
Bliss, Arthur (1891-)	Sonata		Oxford 22.405
Bloch, Ernest (1880-1959)	Suite		GS 29548
	Suite Hebraique		GS 42892
Boccherini, Luigi (1743-1805)	Sonata in C Minor		Carisch
	Sonata in C Minor		Mills 21373
	Sonata in C Minor	Ewerhart-Koch	Schott 4740

SONATAS, SONATINAS, SUITES, DIVERTIMENTOS (Cont'd)

Composer	Title	Editor	Publisher
Boccherini, Luigi (1743-1805)	Sonata no. 3 in G (originally for violoncello and piano)	Alard-Meyer	International
	Sonata no. 6 in A (originally for violoncello and piano)	Katims	International 931
Borris, Siegfried (1906-)	Kleine Suite		Sirius
	Sonate, op. 51		Sirius
Bottze, Will (1925-)	Fantasy Sonata		CFE
Bowen, York (1884-1961)	Sonata no. 1 in C Minor	Tertis	Schott
Brahms, Johannes (1833-1897)	2 Sonatas, op. 120		Peters 3896c
	Sonata in F Minor, op. 120, no. 1	Katims	International
	Sonata in F Minor		Augener
	Sonata in F Minor		BRH
	Sonata in F Minor		Patelson
	Sonata in F Minor		Simrock
	Sonata in E flat, op. 120, no. 2	Katims	International
	Sonata in E flat		Augener
	Sonata in E flat		BRH
	Sonata in E flat		Patelson
	Sonata in E flat		Simrock
	Sonata in E Minor, op. 38 (originally for violoncello and piano	Tertis	Augener
	Sonata in E		International
Bréville, Pierre de (1861-1949)	Sonata		Eschig
Bunin, Revol (1924-)	Sonata, op. 26	Barshai	MZK (MCA No. 2289)
Burton, Eldin	Sonata		CF 04174
Cellier, Alesandre (1883-)	Sonata in G		Salabert
Ceremuga, Josef (1930-)	Sonata elegica		Panton
Chailley, Jacques (1910-)	Sonate		Leduc
Clarke, Rebecca (1886-)	Sonata		Chester
Clementi, Muzio (1752-1832)	Sonatina, op. 36, no. 1 (originally for piano)		Belwin S.I. 52
Connick	Sonata in D Minor		Peters B-015
Corelli, Arcangelo (1653-1713)	Sonata in D Minor	Katims	International 662
	Sonata in D Minor, op. 5, no. 12, "La Folia"	Alard-Dessauer	Schott 946
	Sonata in D Minor, op. 5, no. 12	David-Hermann	International 1018
	Sonata da camera	Forbes-Richardson	Oxford 22.400
Creston, Paul (1906-)	Suite, op. 13		Templeton

Composer	Title	Editor	Publisher
Dahl, Ingolf (1912-)	Divertimento		SPAM
Dallinger	Sonata		Doblinger
Delden, Lex van (1919-)	Suite, op. 4		Donemus (Pet No. D224)
Delius, Frederick (1862-1934)	Sonata no. 2 Sonata no. 3	Tertis Tertis	BH BH
Diabelli, Anton (1781-1858)	Sonatina in A Minor	Baechi	Hug (Pet No. A59)
Dittersdorf, Karl Ditters von (1739-1799)	Sonata in E flat Sonata in E flat Sonata in E flat	Mlynarczyk-Lürmann Schroeder Vieland	Hofmeister BRH International
Eccles, Henry (c1670-1742)	Sonata in G Minor Sonata in G Minor	Katims Klengel	International 441 Peters 4326
Eder, Helmut (1916-)	Sonatina, op. 34, no. 2		Doblinger
Edmunds, Christopher (1899-)	Sonata in D		Novello
Etler, Alvin (1913-)	Sonata (for viola and harpsichord)		AMP
Evett, Robert (1922-)	Sonata		CFE
Fasch, Johann (1688-1758)	Sonata	Doktor	MM
Finke, Fidelio (1891-)	Sonata		BRH
Finney, Ross Lee (1906-)	Sonata Sonata no. 2		Peters 66154 Peters 66253
Flackton, William (1709-1798)	Sonata in C, op. 2, no. 4 Sonata in C, op. 2, no. 4 Sonata in C Minor, op. 2, no. 8 Sonata in D, op. 2, no. 5 Sonata in G, op. 2, no. 6 Sonata in G, op. 2, no. 6 Sonata in C Minor	Bergmann Sabatini Bergmann Sabatini Sabatini Bergmann Cullen	Schott 10261 Doblinger Schott 10957 Doblinger Doblinger Schott 10115 Lengnick (Mil. No. L2010)
Flosman, Oldřich (1925-)	Jesenická suita		Artia
Franck, César (1822-1890)	Sonata in A	Vieland	International
Franck, Maurice (1892-)	Suite		Transatlantiques
Francoeur, Francois (1698-1787)	Sonata no. 4 in E	Alard-Dessauer	International
Fulton, Norman (1909-)	Sonata da Camera		Chester
Fürst, Paul Walter (1926-)	Sonata, op. 33 Sonatina, op. 13		Doblinger Doblinger

147

SONATAS, SONATINAS, SUITES, DIVERTIMENTOS (Cont'd)

Composer	Title	Editor	Publisher
Gauldin, Robert	Sonata Serioso		Tritone
Geissler, Fritz (1921-)	Sonatina		BRH
Genzmer, Harald (1909-)	Sonata in D Sonate no. 2		RE 32 Bärenreiter 3223
Gerster, Ottmar (1897-)	Sonate		Hofmeister
Gideon, Miriam (1906-)	Sonata		CFE
Giordani, Tommaso (c1730-1806)	Sonate in B flat	Ruff	Schott 5951
Glinka, Mikhail (1804-1857)	Sonata in D Minor		MR
Graun, Johann (1703-1771)	Sonata no. 1 in B flat Sonata no. 2 in F Sonata in C Minor	Wolff Wolff Mueller	BRH BRH Sikorski 564
Grazioli, Giovanni (1746-1820	Sonata in F	Marchet	Augener 5569
Grieg, Edvard (1843-1907)	Sonata in A Minor, op. 36 (originally for violoncello and piano) Sonata in A, op. 36	Platz	Peters 2157A International
Hamann, Erich (1898-)	Sonata, op. 33		Doblinger
Hamilton, Iain (1922-)	Sonata, op. 9		Schott
Hammer, Xaver (c1750-1813)	Sonata in D		EdM
Handel, Georg Friedrich (1685-1759)	Sonata in A	David-Hermann	International
	Sonata in A	Forbes-Richardson	Oxford 22.007
	Sonata in C (originally for gamba)	Jensen	International
	Sonata in C	Hoffmann	Schott 4164
	Sonata in E Minor	Courte	Elkan
	Sonata in G Minor	Dart	Schott 10114
	Sonata in G Minor	Katims	International
	Sonata no. 3 (originally for gamba)	Shore	Williams
	Sonata no. 4 (originally for violin and piano)	D'Ambrosio	Ricordi ER 2106
	Sonata no. 4 (originally for violin and piano)	Shore	Williams
	Sonata no. 6 (originally for violin and piano)	Shore	Williams 1401
	Sonata no. 6		MZK
	Sonata no. 10 in G Minor		International
Hanus, Jan (1915-)	Sonatina, op. 37		Artia
Harris, William (1883-)	Suite		Oxford 22.407
Harrison, Julius (1885-1963)	Sonata in C Minor		Lengnick (Mil. No. L2005)

Composer	Title	Editor	Publisher
Harsanyi, Tibor (1898-1954)	Sonata		Heugel
Hartley, Walter (1927-)	Sonata		Interlochen Press
Haydn, Joseph (1732-1809)	Divertimento	Piatigorsky-Elkan	EV
Hemel, Oscar van (1892-)	Sonata		Heuwek
Hennessy, Swan (1866-1929)	Sonata Celtique, op. 62		Eschig
Hindemith, Paul (1895-1963)	Sonate, 1939 Sonate, op. 11, no. 4		Schott 3640 Schott 1976
Holland, Theodore (1878-1947)	Suite in D		BH
Holler, Karl (1907-)	Sonate in E, op. 62		Schott 5847
Holt, Patricia	Suite no. 2		BMI-C
Honneger, Arthur (1892-1955)	Sonata		Eschig
Hook, James (1746-1827)	Sonatina	Applebaum	Belwin S.I. 62
Hruška, Jaromír (1910-)	Sonata		Artia
Hummel, Johann (1778-1837)	Sonata in E flat, op. 5, no. 3 Sonata in E flat, op. 5, no. 3 Sonata	Doktor Lebermann Rood	Doblinger Schott 5954 MM
Hurník, Ilja (1922-)	Sonata		Artia
d'Indy, Vincent (1851-1931)	Sonate en Ré, op. 84		RL
Ireland, John (1879-1962)	Sonata	Tertis	Augener
Ivanov-Radkevich, Nikolay (1904-1962)	Sonata-Poem		MZK (MCA No. 2301)
Jacob, Gordon (1895-)	Sonatina		Novello
Jacobi, Wolfgang (1894-)	Sonata		Sikorski 387
Joubert, John (1927-)	Sonata, op. 6		Novello
Juon, Paul (1872-1940)	Sonata in D, op. 15 Sonata in D, op. 15	Katims	International Lienau (Pet No. R31)
Karg-Elert, Sigfrid (1877-1933)	Sonata, no. 2, op. 139		ZM (Pet No. 2M 1730b)

SONATAS, SONATINAS, SUITES, DIVERTIMENTOS (Cont'd)

Composer	Title	Editor	Publisher
Kaufmann, Armin (1902-)	Sonatine, op. 53		Doblinger
Keldorfer, Robert (1901-)	Sonata		Doblinger
Keller, Homer	Sonata		CFE
Kelley, Robert (1916-)	Sonata		CFE
Kittler, Richard (1924-)	Sonatina		Doblinger
Klaas, Julius (1888-)	Sonata, op. 40		Noetzel (Pet No. N1195)
Koechlin, Charles (1867-1950)	Sonate		Senart
Koringer	Sonatine		Doblinger
Kornauth, Egon (1891-1959)	Sonata in C sharp Minor, op. 3 Sonatina, op. 46a		Doblinger Doblinger
Krenek, Ernst (1900-)	Sonata		Mills
Kriukov, Vladimir (1902-)	Sonata		MZK
Kubizek, Augustin (1918-)	Sonatina, op. 5		Doblinger
Labroca, Marino (1896-)	Suite		SZ
Leclair, Jean Marie (1697-1764)	Sonata "Le Tombeau" (originally for violin)	David-Hermann	International
Legley, Victor (1915-)	Sonata, op. 13		BCM
Locatelli, Pietro (1695-1764)	Sonata in G Minor, op. 6, no. 12 Sonata in G Minor	Doktor David-Hermann	International International
Loeillet, Jean-Baptiste (1680-1730)	Sonata in B flat Sonata in F sharp Minor		International International
Lohse, Fred (1908-)	Sonata		Metropolis
London, Edwin (1929-)	Sonatina		Valley
Lundén, Lennart (1914-1966)	Suite		Nordiska
Makarov, Y.	Sonata, op. 5		MZK (MCA No. 2309)
Mannino, Franco (1924-)	Piccola Sonata		Sonzogno 2871
Mansurian, T.	Sonata		MZK (MCA No. 2310)
Marais, Marin (1656-1728)	Suite in D	Dalton	Peters 6461

Composer	Title	Editor	Publisher
Marcello, Benedetto (1686-1739)	Sonata in E Minor	Marchet	Augener 5574
	Sonata in E Minor	Marchet	International
	Sonata in F	Sosin	MZK 4935
	2 Sonatas, in F and G Minor	Katims	International 855
	2 Sonatas, in G and C	Vieland	International
	Sonata in G	Gibson-Moffat	Schott 1238a
	Sonata in G (for viola and guitar or lute)	Azpiazu	ZM
	Sonata in G Minor, op. 11, no. 4	Piatti-d'Ambrosio	Ricordi 125328
Maros, Rudolf (1917-)	Albanian Suite		Kultura
Martelli, Henri (1895-)	Sonata		Choudens (Pet No. C405)
Martinu, Bohuslav (1809-1959)	Sonata no. 1	Fuchs	AMP
Matys, Jiří (1927-)	Sonata, op. 16		Artia
Matz, Arnold (1904-)	Mixolydian Sonatina		Peters 4608
Mellers, Wilfrid (1914-)	Sonata		Lengnick (Mil No. L2004)
Ménasce, Jacques de (1905-1960)	Sonate en un mouvement		Durand
Mendelssohn, Felix (1809-1847)	Sonata in C Minor		DVM
Meulemans, Arthur (1884-1966)	Sonata		BCM
Mihalovici, Marcel (1898-)	Sonata, op. 47		Heugel
Milhaud, Darius (1892-)	Sonata no. 1 sur des themes inedits et anonymes du XVIII siecle		Heugel
	Sonata no. 2		Heugel
Mohler, Philipp (1908-)	Konzertante Sonata, op. 31		Schott 4490
Mozart, Wolfgang Amadeus (1756-1791)	Divertimento in C	Piatigorsky-Elkan	EV
	Divertimento in F	Courte	UMP
	Sonata in E Minor, K 304 (originally for violin and piano)	Ritter	International
	Sonata in E Minor, K 304	Forbes	Peters 7089
	Sonata in E flat	Courte	UMP
	Sonata in E flat	Courte	Elkan
	Sonatina in C	Piatigorsky-Elkan	Elkan
	Sonatina in F	Courte	Elkan
	Sonatina in G	Courte	Elkan
Mylius, Hermann	Suite in C Minor, op. 30		BRH
Nardini, Pietro (1722-1793)	Sonata no. 1 in B flat	Alard-Dessauer	International

SONATAS, SONATINAS, SUITES, DIVERTIMENTOS (Cont'd)

Composer	Title	Editor	Publisher
Nardini, Pietro (1722-1793)	Sonata in D	Katims	International
	Sonata in F Minor	Zellner	International
Niggeling, Willy (1900-)	Sonata		MV (Pet No. MV 1057)
Onslow, Georges (1784-1853)	Sonata in A, op. 16, no. 3	Höckner	Simrock
Orthel, Leon (1905-)	Sonata, op. 52		Donemus (Pet No. D357)
Overton, Hall (1920-)	Sonata		CFE
Paganini, Niccolo (1782-1840)	Sonata no. 12 (originally for violin and guitar)	Forbes-Richardson	Augener
Palmer, Robert (1915-)	Sonata		Peer
Parris, Robert (1924-)	Sonata		CFE
Paul, Alan (1905-)	Sonata		Bosworth
Pitfield, Thomas (1903-)	Sonatina		Cramer
Podest, Ludvik (1921-)	Suite		Artia
Porpora, Nicola (1686-1768)	Sonata no. 9 in E (originally for violin and clavier)	Alard-Dessauer	International
	Sonata in G (originally for violin and clavier)	David-Hermann	International
Purcell, Henry (1659-1695)	Sonata in G Minor	Forbes-Richardson	Oxford 22.802
Quinet, Fernand (1898-)	Sonate		Senart
Rainier, Priaulx (1903-)	Sonata		Schott 10410
Raphael, Günther (1903-1960)	Sonata in E flat, op. 13		BRH
	Sonata no. 2, op. 80		BRH
Rawsthorne, Alan (1905-)	Sonata		Oxford 22.406
Reger, Max (1873-1916)	Sonata in B flat, op. 107 (originally for clarinet and piano)		BB
Reiter, Albert (1905-)	Sonata		Doblinger
Rettich, William	Suite in Old Style, op. 40c		Novello
Ribári, Antal	Sonata	Lukács	Kultura
Ribollet, Albert	Suite, op. 23		Leduc
Richardson, Alan (1904-)	Sonata, op. 21		Augener

Composer	Title	Editor	Publisher
Roger, Kurt (1895-1966)	Irish Sonata, op. 37		FDH
Rogers, William (1921-)	Sonatina		BMI-C
Rosseau, Norbert (1907-)	Sonatina, op. 41		BCM
Rubinstein, Anton (1829-1894)	Sonata in F Minor, op. 49		BRH
Rudzinski, Witold (1913-)	Sonata		PWM
Ryelandt, Joseph (1870-1965)	Sonata op. 73		BCM
Sapp, Allen (1922-)	Sonata no. 1		CFE
Schiff, Helmut (1918-)	Sonata		Doblinger
Schmidt, William (1926-)	Sonata		Western
Schoendlinger, Anton (1919-)	Sonata		BRH
Schollum, Robert (1913-)	Sonata op. 42, no. 2		Doblinger
	Sonatine op. 57, no. 2		Doblinger
Schubert, Franz (1797-1828)	Sonata in A (originally for arpeggione and piano)	Katims	International
	Sonata in A (originally for arpeggione and piano)	Platz	Doblinger
	Sonata in A (originally for arpeggione and piano)	Rostal	Schott 6064
	Sonata Movement from Trio in B flat	Forbes	Augener 18584R
	3 Sonatinas, op. 137 (originally for violin and piano)	Forbes	Augener 7571a
	Sonatina in D, op. 137, no. 1 (originally for violin and piano)	Ritter	International
Schumann, Robert (1810-1856)	Märchenbilder, op. 113	Schradieck	GS L415
	Märchenbilder, op. 113		BRH
	Märchenbilder, op. 113		Peters 2372
Senaillé, Jean Baptiste (1687-1730)	Sonata no. 9, op. 5	Morgan	Augener 7405a
Sendrey, Albert (1911-)	Sonata		EV
Shebalin, Vissarion (1902-1963)	Sonata		MZK (MCA No. 2323)
Sherman, Elna	Sonata Lyrica		CFE
Siegl, Otto (1896-)	Sonata no. 1, op. 41		Doblinger
	Sonata no. 2 in E flat, op. 103		Doblinger
Skorzeny, Fritz (1900-1965)	Sonate		Doblinger
Smith, Leland	Sonata		CFE

Composer	Title	Editor	Publisher
Soproni, József	Sonatina		Kultura
Sprongl, Norbert (1892-)	Sonata, op. 115		Doblinger
Stamitz, Johann (1717-1757)	Sonata		MZK
Stamitz, Karl (1745-1801)	Sonata in B flat	Lebermann	Schott 5955
	Sonata in B flat	Lenzewski	Vieweg
	Sonata in B flat	Primrose	International
	Sonata in E Minor, op. 6	Borissovsky	International
Stanford, Charles (1852-1924)	Sonata		STB
Stepanov, Lev (1908-)	Sonata		MZK (MCA No. 2328)
Stevens, Halsey (1908-)	Serenade		Mercury
	Suite		Peer
	Suite		Peters 6031
Stevens, James (1927-)	Four Movements and a Coda		EDW
Still, Robert (1910-)	Sonata no. 2		Chester
Subotnick, Morton	Sonata		MM
Suchy, Frantisek (1891-)	Suite		Artia
Tartini, Giuseppe (1692-1770)	Sonata in C Minor	Forbes-Richardson	Oxford 22.808
	Sonata in D	Hermann	International 1880
	Sonata no. 2 in F	Alard-Dessauer	International 941
Telemann, Georg Philipp (1681-1767)	Sonata in A Minor	Dolmetsch-Wood	Schott 10357
	Sonata in A Minor	Schulz-Vieland	International
	Sonata in B flat	Ruff	Schott 5652
	Sonata in D		BVP (Pet No. B-016)
	Sonata in D		International
	Sonata in G	Ruff	WM (Pet No. WM62)
	Suite in D	Bergmann-Forbes	Schott 10196
Torrandell	Sonate, op. 21		Salabert
Trevani, Francesco	3 Sonatas	Stierhof	Doblinger
Trexler, Georg (1903-)	Sonatina		BRH
Valentini, Giuseppe (c1681-c1740)	Sonata no. 10 in E	Rakowski	PWM
Van de Vate, Nancy (1931-)	Sonata		Tritone
Vaňhal, Jan (1739-1813)	Sonata		International

Composer	Title	Editor	Publisher
Vassilenko, Sergey (1872-1956)	Sonata, op. 46		MZK (MCA No. 2339)
Veracini, Francesco (1690-1750)	Sonata in E Minor		International
Verrall, John (1908-)	Sonata no. 2		Peters 6587
Vigueri	Sonatina in C		Belwin S.I. 50
Vivaldi, Antonio (c1669-1741)	6 Sonatas (originally for violoncello and piano)	Primrose	International
	Sonata in A	David-Hermann	International
	Sonata in A Minor	Primrose	International
	Sonata in B flat	Primrose	International
	Sonata in G Minor	Katims	International
Voormolen, Alexander (1895-)	Sonata (1953)		Donemus (Pet No. D87)
Walthew, Richard (1872-1951)	Serenade-Sonata in F Minor		Williams (Mil No. W1419)
	Sonata in D		STB
Webber, Lloyd	Sonatina		Augener
Weber, Carl Maria von (1786-1826)	Serenata, op. 3, no. 1	Forbes	Schott
Weiner, László	Sonata		Kultura
Weyruch, Johannes (1897-)	Passion Sonata, Herzliebster Zesu		Peters 13-003
Winkler, Alexander (1865-1935)	Sonata, op. 10		MZK (MCA No. 2346)
Wood, Joseph (1915-)	Sonata		CFE
Woollett, Henri (1864-1936)	Sonata no. 5		Salabert
Wunderer, Alexander (1877-1955)	Sonate, op. 21		Doblinger
Zeisl, Eric (1905-1959)	Sonata in A Minor	Reher	Doblinger

IV SELECTED WORKS WITH VARIOUS INSTRUMENTS

Composer	Title	Editor	Publisher
Bach, Johann Sebastian (1685-1750)	Brandenburg Concerto no. 6 for 2 violas and piano		Hinrichsen
	15 Terzetti for 2 violins and viola	David	International
Bach, Karl Philipp Emanuel (1714-1788)	6 Sonatas for viola, violoncello, and piano		International
	Trio Sonata in F for 2 violas and piano	Brandts-Buys	Schott
Bach, Wilhelm Friedemann (1710-1784)	3 Duets for 2 violas	Altemark	BRH
Beethoven, Ludwig van (1770-1827)	Duet "Eyeglasses Obbligato" for viola and violoncello		International, Peters

Composer	Title	Editor	Publisher
Beethoven, Ludwig van (1770-1827)	3 Duets for violin and viola	Hermann-Pagels	International
	12 German Dances for 2 violins and viola		International
	Serenade in D, op. 8 for violin, viola and violoncello		BRH, International, Peters 3375A
	Serenade, op. 25 for flute, violin and viola		BRH, International, Peters
	Trio, op. 87 for 3 violas	Tertis	Bosworth
	Trio, op. 87 for 2 violins and viola		BRH, International
	6 Trios for violin, viola, and violoncello		Peters 194
Benjamin, Arthur (1893-1960)	Romantic Fantasy for violin, viola, and piano		BH
Berger, Melvin	3 14th Century Dances for viola and tambour		MCA
Bloch, Ernest (1880-1959)	Concertino for flute, viola, and piano		GS
Brahms, Johannes (1833-1897)	2 Songs, op. 91, for alto, viola, and piano		Peters, Simrock
Castelnuovo-Tedesco, Mario (1895-)	Sonata for viola and violoncello		Mills
Cherubini, Luigi (1760-1842)	2 Fugues for 2 violas	Twinn	Augener
Colgrass, Michael	Variations for viola and percussion		M Per
Cowell, Henry (1897-1965)	Variations on Thirds for 2 violas and orchestra		Peters
Debussy, Claude (1862-1918)	Sonata for Flute, Viola, and Harp		Durand
Dittersdorf, Karl Ditters von (1739-1799)	Divertimento for violin, viola, and violoncello		International
	Symphonie Concertante in D for viola, double-bass, and piano		International
Dohnányi, Ernst (1877-1960)	Serenade, op. 10, for violin, viola and violoncello		International, Doblinger
Dvořák, Antonín (1841-1904)	Terzetto in C, op. 74, for 2 violins and viola		Peters
Fine, Irving (1914-1962)	Fantasia for violin, viola, and violoncello		Mills
Gerschefski, Edwin (1909-)	Workout for 2 violins and 2 violas		CFE
Handel, Georg Friedrich (1685-1759)	Passacaglia for violin and viola	Halvorsen	Hansen 507
	Sarabande for violin and viola	Halvorsen	Hansen 508
Haydn, Joseph (1732-1809)	12 Easy Trios for 2 violins and viola 2 vol.		International
	6 Sonatas for violin and viola	Bonelli	Doblinger
Haydn, Michael (1737-1801)	4 Sonatas for violin and viola 2 vol.	Altmann	BRH
Hindemith, Paul (1895-1963)	Duet for viola and violoncello		Schott
	Trio no. 1, op. 34 for violin, viola, and violoncello		Schott
	Trio no. 2 for violin, viola and violoncello		Schott
Hoffmeister, Franz Anton (1754-1812)	Duet in D for violin and viola	Primrose	International

156

Composer	Title	Editor	Publisher
Hummel, Johann (1778-1837)	Trio in E flat for 2 violas and violoncello Trio in G for 2 violas and violoncello		Peters 4862A Peters 4862B
Jacobson	3 Varieties for 3 violas		Mills
Kodály, Zoltán (1882-)	Serenade, op. 12, for 2 violins and viola		UE 6655
Martinu, Bohuslav (1890-1959)	3 Madrigals for violin and viola		BH
Massias, Gérard (1933-)	Tjurunga for 3 violas		Jobert
Mazas, Jacques-Féréol (1782-1849)	Duos Concertante, op. 71, for 2 violas 2 vol.		Cranz
Mozart, Wolfgang Amadeus (1756-1791)	Divertimento no. 3 in C for 2 violins and viola Divertimento in E flat, K. 563, for violin, viola, and violoncello 2 Duets, K. 423 and K. 424, for violin and viola 12 Duets, K. 487 Sinfonia Concertante in E flat, K. 364, for violin, viola, and orchestra	Klengel	BRH Bärenreiter, BRH, International, Peters BRH, GS, International, Peters, UE Bärenreiter, BRH, FC International BH, BRH, Broude, GS, GT, Kalmus
Paganini, Niccolò (1782-1840)	Terzetto Concerto in D for viola, violoncello, and guitar		ZM
Partos, Ödön	Agada for viola, piano, and percussion		IMI
Pisk, Paul (1893-)	Ballade for 6 violas		CFE
Piston, Walter (1894-)	Duo for viola and violoncello		AMP
Rolla, Alessandro (1757-1841)	Duo Concertante for violin and viola		EdM
Schickele, Peter (1935-)	Windows, 3 Pieces for viola and guitar		Tetra
Schoenberg, Arnold (1874-1951)	Trio, op. 45 for violin, viola, and violoncello		Bomart
Schumann, Gerhard (1914-)	Allegro for 4 violas		Sirius
Spies, Claudio	Viopiacem (1969)		BH
Stamitz, Karl (1746-1801)	3 Duets for 2 violas 6 Duets, op. 18, for violin and viola 2 vol.	Lebermann Ott	Schott Leuckart
Sterkel, Johann (1750-1817)	3 Duets for 2 violas		Hofmeister
Telemann, Georg Philipp (1681-1767)	Sonata in A Minor for viola, guitar, or lute	Azpiazu	ZM
Toch, Ernst (1887-)	Divertimento, op. 37, no. 2, for violin and viola Serenade, op. 25, for 2 violins and viola		Schott MCA
Townsend, Douglas (1921-)	Duo, op. 5, for 2 violas		Peters 6038
Walzel, Leopold (1902-)	5 Bagatelles for viola and double bass		Doblinger

V VIOLA D'AMORE

Composer	Title	Editor	Publisher
Ariosti, Attilio (1660-1740)	2 Sonatas for viola d'amour and piano	Sabatini Renzo	Santis 980
Bach, Johann Sebastian (1685-1750)	Bach Studies	Spindler-Drechsel	Hofmeister
Borris, Siegfried (1906-)	Sonata, op. 105, for viola d'amour and klavier		Sirius
Casadesus, Henri (1879-1947)	24 Préludes pour Viole d'Amour et Clavecin Technique de la Viole d'Amour		Salabert Salabert
Corras, A.	Méthode de Viole d'Amour Minuetto ancien		Salabert Salabert
Ghedini, Giorgio (1892-)	Musica da concerto for viola d'amore and orchestra		Ricordi
Hammer, Xaver (1750-1813)	Sonata in D for viola d'amore and piano (see COLLECTIONS OF SOLOS, Meyer, editor)		Peters 3816
Hindemith, Paul (1895-1963)	Kleine Sonate, op. 25, no. 2, for viola d'amore and piano		Schott 2079
Hofmann, Wolfgang	Sonatine for viola d'amore and harpsichord		Sirius
Loeffler, Charles (1861-1935)	La Mort de Tintagiles		GS
Martin, Frank (1890-)	Sonata da Chiesa for viola d'amore and string orchestra		UE 12118
Quantz, Johann (1697-1773)	Trio in F for viola d'amore, flute, and piano		ZM (Pet No. ZM 1088)
Shirley, Paul	The Study of the Viola d'Amore		Peters 6143
Stumpf, Karl	New School for Viola d'Amore		OBV
Telemann, Georg Philipp (1681-1767)	Concerto in E for flute, oboe d'amore, viola d'amore, and piano		Peters 5885
Toeschi, Giovanni (1727-1800)	Sonata	Newlin-Stumpf	Doblinger
Telemann	Concerto in D for viola d'amore, guitar, and string quartet		ZM (Pet No. ZM 1320)
Vivaldi, Antonio (1669-1741)	Concerto in A	Townsend	Ricordi 2532
	Concerto in A, F. II no. 1, for viola d'amore and string orchestra	Malipiero	Ricordi PR 714
	Concerto in D Minor, F. II no. 2, for viola d'amore and string orchestra	Malipiero	Ricordi PR 721
	Concerto in D Minor, F. II no. 3, for viola d'amore and string orchestra	Malipiero	Ricordi PR 722
	Concerto in D Minor, F. II no. 4, for viola d'amore and string orchestra	Malipiero	Ricordi PR 723
	Concerto in D, F. II no. 5, for viola d'amore and string orchestra	Malipiero	Ricordi PR 987
	Concerto in A, F. II no. 6, for viola d'amore and string orchestra	Malipiero	Ricordi PR 991
	Concerto for viola d'amore and piano	Borisovsky	MZK (MCA No. 2345)
Waefelghem, Louis van (1840-1908)	Romance Soir d'automne		Durand Durand

DIRECTORY OF MUSIC PUBLISHERS

Code	Publisher	American Agent or Parent Company
ABRSM	Associated Board of Royal Schools of Music	Belwin-Mills Publishing Corp.
AMP	Associated Music Publishers, Inc. 609 Fifth Avenue New York, N.Y. 10017	
Amphion	Editions Amphion	Belwin-Mills Publishing Corp.
Artia	Artia	Boosey & Hawkes, Inc.
Augener	Augener, Ltd.	Galaxy Music Corp.
Bärenreiter	Bärenreiter-Verlag	Broude Brothers
BB	Bote and Bock	Associated Music Publishers, Inc.
BCM	Belgian Centre of Music Documentation	Henri Elkan Music Publisher
Belwin	Belwin-Mills Publishing Corp. Melville Long Island, N.Y. 11746	
Belaieff	M. P. Belaieff	Boosey & Hawkes, Inc.
BH	Boosey & Hawkes, Inc. Oceanside, N.Y. 11572	
Big 3	Big 3 Music Corp. 1350 Avenue of the Americas New York, N.Y. 10019	
Billaudot	Editions Billaudot	Southern Music Company, Texas
BMC	Boston Music Company Boylston Street Boston, Mass. 02116	
BMI-C	BMI-Canada, Ltd.	Associated Music Publishers, Inc.
Bomart	Bomart Music Publications	Associated Music Publishers, Inc.
Bongiovanni	Casa Musicale Francesco Bongiovanni	Belwin-Mills Publishing Corp.
Bosworth	Bosworth & Company, Inc.	Belwin-Mills Publishing Corp.
Bourne	Bourne Company 136 West 52nd Street New York, N.Y. 10019	
BRH	Breitkopf & Hartel	Associated Music Publishers, Inc.
Brodt	Brodt Music Company 1409 E. Independence Blvd. Charlotte, N.C. 28201	
Broude	Broude Brothers, Inc. 56 West 45th Street New York, N.Y. 10036	
Brown	Robert B. Brown Music Company 1815 N. Kenmore Avenue Hollywood, Calif.	
BVP	Broekmans & Van Poppel	C. F. Peters Corp.
Carisch	Carisch	Belwin-Mills Publishing Corp.
CF	Carl Fischer, Inc. 56-62 Cooper Square New York, N.Y. 10003	

Code	Publisher	American Agent or Parent Company
CFE	Composers Facsimile Edition 170 West 74th Street New York, N.Y. 10023	
Choudens	Choudens	C. F. Peters Corp.
Chappell	Chappell & Company, Inc. 609 Fifth Avenue New York, N.Y. 10017	
Chappell-L	Chappell & Company, Ltd.	Chappell & Company, Inc.
Chester	J. & W. Chester, Ltd.	Belwin-Mills Publishing Corp.
Cole	M. M. Cole Publishing Company 251 E. Grand Avenue Chicago, Illinois 60611	
Concert	Concert Music Publishing Company 5004 South Jefferson Avenue St. Louis, Missouri 63118	
Cor	Cor Publishing Company 67 Bell Place Massapequa, Long Island, N.Y. 11758	
CP	Composers Press	Southern Music Publishing Company, Texas
Cramer	J. B. Cramer & Company, Ltd.	Brodt Music Company
Cranz	Editions A. Cranz	Henri Elkan Music Publisher Rubank, Inc.
Curci	Edizioni Curci	Big 3 Music Corp.
Curwen	J. Curwen & Sons, Ltd.	G. Schirmer, Inc.
Deiss	Deiss	Belwin-Mills Publishing Corp.
DM	Samfundet til Udgivelse af dansk Musik Kronprinsessegade 26 Copenhagen K. Denmark	
Doblinger	Ludwig Doblinger Verlag	Associated Music Publishers, Inc.
Donemus	Donemus	C. F. Peters Corp.
Durand	Durand & Cie	Elkan-Vogel Company, Inc.
DVM	Deutsche Verlag fur Musik	Associated Music Publishers, Inc.
ECIC	Editorial Cooperativa Interamericana de Compositores	Southern Music Publishing Company, N.Y.
EdM	Edition Musicus–N.Y., Inc. 333 West 52nd Street New York, N.Y.	
EDW	Edition Modern Musikverlag Hans Wewerka Franz-Josef-Strasse 2 Munich, Germany	Boston Music Company
Elkan	Henri Elkan Music Publisher 1316 Walnut Street Philadelphia, Pa. 19107	
Eschig	Editions Max Eschig	Associated Music Publishers, Inc.
Etling	Forest R. Etling 1790 Joseph Court Elgin, Illinois 60120	

Code	Publisher	American Agent or Parent Company
Eulenberg	Edition Eulenberg	C. F. Peters Corp.
EV	Elkan-Vogel Company, Inc. Division of Theodore Presser Company Presser Place Bryn Mawr, Pa. 19010	
FC	Franco Colombo Publications Division of Belwin-Mills Rockville Centre Long Island, N.Y. 11571	
FDH	Francis Day & Hunter, Ltd.	Big 3 Music Corp.
Fillmore	Fillmore Music House	Carl Fischer, Inc.
FitzSimons	H. T. Fitzsimons Company 615 N. La Salle Street Chicago, Ill. 60610	
Forlivesi	Forlivesi & Company	Belwin-Mills Publishing Corp.
Fox	Sam Fox Publishing Company 1841 Broadway New York, N.Y. 10019	
Galaxy	Galaxy Music Corp. 2121 Broadway New York, N.Y. 10023	
Galliard	Galliard, Ltd.	Galaxy Music Corp.
Gaudet	Gaudet	Belwin-Mills Publishing Corp.
Gehrmans	Carl Gehrmans Musikforlag	Boosey & Hawkes, Inc. Elkan-Vogel Company, Inc. Mills Music, Inc.
General	General Music Publishing Company, Inc.	Boston Music Company
Gerig	Musikverlag Hans Gerig	Big 3 Music Corp. MCA Music
Gilles	Gilles	Belwin-Mills Publishing Corp.
Grahl	H. L. Grahl, Taunus-Verlag	C. F. Peters Corp.
GS	G. Schirmer, Inc. 609 Fifth Avenue New York, N.Y. 10017	
GT	Goodwin & Tabb, Ltd.	Belwin-Mills Publishing Corp. C. F. Peters Corp.
Hamelle	Hamelle & Cie	Elkan-Vogel Company, Inc.
Hansen	Musik-Forlag Wilhelm Hansen	G. Schirmer, Inc.
Hänssler	Hänssler Verlag	C. F. Peters
Heugel	Heugel & Cie	Theodore Presser Company
Hieber	Max Hieber Musikverlag	C. F. Peters Corp.
Highgate	Highgate Press	Galaxy Music Corp.
Hinrichsen	Hinrichsen Edition, Ltd.	C. F. Peters Corp.
Hofmeister	Friedrich Hofmeister	Associated Music Publishers, Inc.
Hug	Hug & Company	C. F. Peters Corp.
IMI	Israeli Music Institute	Boosey & Hawkes, Inc.

Code	Publisher	American Agent or Parent Company
IMP	Israeli Music Publications	Belwin-Mills Publishing Corp.
Impero	Impero Verlag	Theodore Presser Company
Interlochen Press	Interlochen Press National Music Camp Interlochen, Mich. 49643	
International	International Music Company 509 Fifth Avenue New York, N.Y. 10017	
Jobert	Editions Jean Jobert	Elkan-Vogel Company, Inc.
Kalmus	Edwin F. Kalmus 1345 New York Avenue Huntington Station, L.I., N.Y. 11746	
Kjos	Neil A. Kjos Music Company 525 Busse Highway Park Ridge, Illinois 60068	
Kneusslin	Kneusslin	C. F. Peters Corp.
Kultura	Kultura	Boosey & Hawkes, Inc.
Leduc	Alphonse Leduc & Cie	Brodt Music Company Edward B. Marks Music Corp. Elkan-Vogel Company, Inc.
Lemonie	Henry Lemonie & Cie	Elkan-Vogel Company, Inc.
Lengnick	Alfred Lengnick & Company Ltd.	Mills Music Publishers, Inc.
Leuckart	F. E. C. Leuckart Musikverlag	Associated Music Publishers, Inc.
Lienau	Robert Lienau Musikverlag	C. F. Peters Corp.
Lyche	Lyche	C. F. Peters Corp.
Markert	John Markert & Company 141 West 15th Street New York, N.Y. 10011	
Marks	Edward B. Marks Music Corp. 136 West 52nd Street New York, N.Y. 10011	
Mathot	A. Z. Mathot	Belwin-Mills Publishing Corp.
MCA	MCA Music 435 Hudson Street New York, N.Y. 10014	
Mel Bay	Mel Bay Publications, Inc. 107 West Jefferson Avenue Kirkwood, Mo. 63122	
Mercury	Mercury Music Corp. 17 West 60th Street New York, N.Y. 10023	
Metropolis	Editions Metropolis	Henri Elkan Music Publisher
Mills	Mills Music, Inc. Division of Belwin-Mills Rockville Centre Long Island, N.Y. 11571	
MM	McGinnis & Marx 201 West 86th Street, Apt. 706 New York, N.Y. 10024	

Code	Publisher	American Agent or Parent Company
Möseler	Möseler Publishing House Wolfenbuttel, W. Germany	
Mowbray	Mowbray Music Publishers	Theodore Presser Company
M Per	Music for Percussion 17 West 60 St. New York, N.Y. 10023	
MPH	Music Publishers Holding Corp. 488 Madison Avenue New York, N.Y. 10022	
MR	Musica Rara	Rubank, Inc.
MV	Mitteldeutscher Verlag	C. F. Peters Corp.
MZK	Mezhdunarodnaya Kniga Music Publishers of the USSR	MCA Music
Nagels	Nagels Verlag	Associated Music Publishers, Inc.
Noetzel	Noetzel	C. F. Peters Corp.
Nordiska	A. B. Nordiska Musikforlaget Fack 8 Stockholm, Sweden	
Norsk	Norsk Musikforlag	Associated Music Publishers, Inc.
Novello	Novello & Company, Ltd.	Belwin-Mills Publishing Corp.
OBV	Oesterrichischer Bundesverlag	Associated Music Publishers, Inc.
Omega	Omega Music Company 19 West 44th Street New York, N.Y. 10016	
Oxford	Oxford University Press, Inc. 200 Madison Avenue New York, N.Y. 10016	
Panton	Panton Verlag	C. F. Peters Corp.
Patelson	Joseph Patelson Music House 158 West 56th Street New York, N.Y. 10019	
Paxton	W. Paxton 7 Company, Ltd.	Belwin-Mills Publishing Corp.
Peer	Peer International Corp. 1619 Broadway New York, N.Y. 10019	
Peters	C. F. Peters Corp. 373 Park Avenue South New York, N.Y. 10016	
Prentice-Hall	Prentice-Hall, Inc. Englewood Cliffs, N.J.	
Presser	Theodore Presser Company Presser Place Bryn Mawr, Pa. 19010	
Presto	Presto Music Service Box 10704 Tampa, Florida	

Code	Publisher	American Agent or Parent Company
Pro Art	Pro Art Publications, Inc. 469 Union Avenue Westbury L.I., N.Y. 11590	
Pro Musica	Pro Musica Verlag Karl-Liebknecht-Strasse 12 701 Leipzig, Germany	
PWM	Polskie Wydawnictwo Muzyczne	Marks
RE	Ries & Erler Musikverlag	C. F. Peters Corp.
Ricordi Ricordi-BA Ricordi-Paris	G. Ricordi & Company	Belwin-Mills Publishing Corp.
Ricard	Ricard	Franco Colombo Publications
Robbins	Robbins Music Corp. 1350 Avenue of the Americas New York, N.Y. 10019	
RL	Rouart-Lerolle et Cie	Belwin-Mills Publishing Corp.
Rubank	Rubank, Inc. 16215 NW 15th Avenue Miami, Fla. 33169	
Salabert	Editions Salabert	Belwin-Mills Publishing Corp.
Santis	Edizioni de Santis	Belwin-Mills Publishing Corp.
SB	Shapiro, Bernstein & Company, Inc. 666 Fifth Avenue New York, N.Y. 10019	
Schott	Schott & Company, Ltd.	Belwin-Mills Publishing Corp.
Senart	Maurice Senart	Belwin-Mills Publishing Corp.
Seraphic	Seraphic Press 1501 South Layton Blvd. Milwaukee, Wisc.	
Shawnee	Shawnee Press, Inc. Delaware Water Gap, Pa. 18327	
Sikorski	Musikverlage Hans Sikorski	Belwin-Mills Publishing Corp.
Simrock	N. Simrock	Associated Music Publishers, Inc.
Sirius	Sirius-Verlag Berlin Wiclefstrasse 67 1 Berlin NW 21, Germany	
SMP	Southern Music Publishing Company 1619 Broadway New York, N.Y. 10019	
Soc	Societe Anonyme D'Editions et de Musique 7 Rue Gambetta Nancy, France	
Sonzogno	Casa Musicale Sonzogno	Belwin-Mills Publishing Corp.
Southern, Texas	Southern Music Company P.O. Box 329 San Antonio, Texas	

Code	Publisher	American Agent or Parent Company
SP	Sprague-Coleman, Inc. 62 West 45th Street New York, N.Y.	
SPAM	Society for the Publication of American Music	Theodore Presser Company
Spratt	Jack Spratt Music Company 77 West Broad STreet Stamford, Conn.	
STB	Stainer & Bell, Ltd.	Galaxy Music Corp.
Summy-Birchard	Summy-Birchard Company Evanston, Illinois 60204	
SZ	Edizioni Suvini Zerboni	MCA Music
Templeton	Templeton Publishing Company, Inc.	Shawnee Press Inc.
Tetra	Tetra Music Corp.	Broude
Thompson	Gordon V. Thompson	Big Three Music Corp.
Transatlantiques	Editions Musicales Transatlantiques	Theodore Presser Company
Tritone	Tritone Press	Theodore Presser Company
UE	Universal Edition	Associated Music Publishers, Inc.
UMP	University Music Press	Sam Fox Publishing Co.
Universal	Universal Musical Instrument Company 723 Braodway New York, N.Y.	
Valley	New Valley Music Press Sage Hall 3 Northampton, Mass. 01060	
Varitone	Varitone, Inc. 545 Fifth Avenue New York, N.Y.	
Vieweg	Chr. Friedrich Vieweg	C. F. Peters Corp.
Wehman	Wehman Brothers 156 Main Street Hackensack, N.J.	
Western	Western International Music 2859 Holt Avenue Los Angeles, Calif. 90034	
Williams	Joseph Williams, Ltd.	Galaxy Music Corp.
Willis	Willis Music Company 440 Main Street Cincinnati, Ohio 45201	
Witmark	M. Witmark & Sons	Music Publishers Holding Corp.
WM	Willy Müller	C. F. Peters Corp.
Zanibon	Zanibon Edition	Belwin-Mills Publishing Corp. C. F. Peters Corp.
ZM	Wilhelm Zimmermann Musikverlag	C. F. Peters Corp.